The Darkside

D1510647

The Darkside

Chronicling the Young Black Experience

Robert Scoop Jackson

The Noble Press, Inc., Chicago

Cover Design by Nobodez Design
Cover Concept by Brad Samuels
Interior by P/R Design Group

Printed in the United States of America

Library of Congress
Cataloguing-in-Publication-Data

Jackson, Robert
    Darkside:chronicling the black experience/robert jackson
p.   cm.
ISBN 1-879360-40-3
1. Afro-Americans-Social Life and Customs

The Noble Press, Inc.
1020 South Wabash Avenue
Chicago, IL 60605

Dedication

This book is dedicated to my wife, Red,
and our son, "Furious"

THE DARKSIDE
Table of Contents

Boy in the Hood

THE DEVIL
MADE ME DO IT

For years I've been a fan. Not-only-the-hair-club-president-I'm-also-a-subscriber type of shit. Hiphop, the whole culture, from Zulu to Zhane, was like blood flowing through my veins. On October 6, I received a fax. The editorial staff of *The Source* was outta there! Oh holy snap! Amidst some ill-odyssey, eight brothas and sistahs (excluding Carter Harris who is white, but down) did the Black thang (the Jordan thang...) by leaving the plantation that made them large and paid their bills.

Hiphop hoomuthafk'nray! We back to our roots, grabbing some control over what we initially created. Even though *The Source* was never really a "Black" magazine, it existed due to Black creativity and ingenuity. So for eight people to do the trick at once (with no severance pay or secured employment in the wings), there musta been some madness goin' down.

To make a long story make sense, David Mays (publisher of *The Source*, and caucasian) pissed off James Bernard (editor of *The Source*, and negroid). Some personal shit was said, some personal shit was done. Lives were threatened; Bernard called mutiny. "Mr. Mays' actions and subsequent comments smack of plantation-style management (i.e. white bossman, Black worker slaves) and are unacceptable in any situation," Bernard wrote in an open letter. Mays retaliated in an "When All Hell Breaks Loose" article in *Rap Sheet*. Oh shit, a race riot! Hiphop was in the middle of its first civil war. God bless Amerikkka.

Then Tonya Pendelton, music editor for *YSB*, went on a midnight run like DeNiro. She rounded up 51 writers and magazine editors to publicly support *The Source* staff walk-out. Of course, I was on the list. "Fk *The Source*!" was the battle cry. This shit was gettin'-good...

Phone rings. It's *The Source*. They need writers. Ha. Bet that. I ain't no scab, second-hand freelance servant. I'm for real. Plus, I don't believe in workin' for white folks, especially those who dog Black folks. They must not have seen my name on that list. "Hell no!" I screamed. "Fk that and fk you!"

"One story. $300?"

"Lemme get back to you."

Phone rings again. It's Common Sense, pissed about his album review in *The Source*. "Fk them," he says.

"Yeah," says I.

His entire career is in jeopardy because of one bad review (that's the power *The Source* can have). He needs me to hook him up. That's my nigga, so whatever he needs.

Phone rings. DAMN! You know who. Why me? Why is this now the worst time for a nigga to be Black? Why in the hell is the magazine I've been trying to get with finally calling me when it's "scab time?" Why hasn't anybody from the "editorial walk-out staff" called me to thank me for my support? Why haven't they started their own magazine? Why do I feel that the right thing to do is what's in the best interest of Common Sense (and Chicago hiphop for that matter)? Why do I feel the white thing to do is to jump at the opportunity to get in *The Source*? Why can't *VIBE* call, put me on, and eliminate all of this madness? Why do I feel like my life's credibility is going to be judged by the chicken-shit decision I make? What's a Black man to do?

The Source, January 1995, page 32, issue No.64. I sold out. Big time! Too young to be an "uncle," I now dub myself "nephew Tom." I'm the new Clarence Thomas of hiphop. No more "Blacker- than-thou" front. I'm open like an Asian mini-market. Doing the story for *The Source* made me feel good about "lookin' out" for my nig' Common Sense, but I also feel like one of the brothas I love to hate. I gotta watch my back, I think I'm about to get dropped. I didn't want to, but the devil made me do it. I think I just ended my chances of getting in a Spike Lee movie and just became a joke on "Def Jam."

So who am I? What have I become? Was my soul stolen, or did I sell it myself? Where's my check? I haven't heard from *The Source* since the story ran. Maybe they just wanted to prove a point, show us Black folks we ain't as strong as we think. I need help; we need help. Yeah, Black is beautiful, but sometimes all of the beauty in the world can't save a nigga's soul. If you see mine, somewhere in New York, rescue it. Take it to Sylvia's for some soul food. Then strangle it. The last thing we need is another non-Black soul working for the white man. Trust me, I know.

4

A HERO AIN'T NOTHING BUT A SANDWICH

an autobio-essay

Earlier this year I was honored by a large Chicago newspaper *(Chicago Sun-Times)* as a "Neighborhood Hero." Here I am, a young Black man living in Amerikkka, appearing in a white newspaper—and I didn't shoot or kill anybody? Something must be wrong. Receiving public recognition for hard work is something unfamiliar to brothas, unless we're athletes or entertainers. Outside of that, the only time you see young brothas getting recognized is on "Cops" or "Court TV."

But here I am getting props for being a "together brotha." I'm dreamin' and I can't wake up, right? If I'm a hero, why do white people walk a little faster when they see me or clutch their purses a little tighter when I'm downtown paying "rent" to the phone company? Don't they read the paper?!? Oh no, I'm the one they fear. I'm the young Black man with his own business that doesn't rely on "outside" support to help him survive. Damn, I forgot. I'm also the brotha who intellectually manhandled one of their liberal representatives on a political talk show one Sunday morning. I'm also the brotha that used to work for a white radio station and left the instant I got an assignment from *The Final Call.* Hero? To "them," I don't think so.

So now I have juice, right? Wrong! How come the brothas on the block "tense" up when we walk past one another? Why do I hear, "Nigga, you ain't all that" from members of the neighborhood where I grew up? Yo, don't they read the paper? Dammit, I forgot. I'm the only nigga in my neighborhood to break camp, go to a Black university—and finish! And yeah, I'm the same "mark" that traded 40's and 12's because malt in the liq was killin' my brain cells. "Little Nigga Turned Too Good," that's what they call me. Hero? Hell no. I guess you can't be large by yourself.

Three months have passed, and they've branded a label on my ass. Hero. Don't own a cape and my Timberlands can't fly, but I'm still...Supernigga.

The truth remains that I'm still me, blacker than the space between the stars. White America, for some reason, usually has a hand in determining our Black heroes. Most of them turn out to be handkerchief-head negroes who have removed themselves from the hood and other Black communities. That works for white America, but choosing me was not a good move on their part. See, I'm the brotha they have to hate. Acknowledging me for the work I've done on the "Black Planet" is good for other Blacks to see—that's it! Heroes save people. I'm just trying to stay Black in the eyes of those who can truly see: Black people.

Reality tells me though, that I could "catch one" in the chest just like the next young ruffneck hangin' on the block. But yo, I'm a hero. I'm not supposed to think that, right? My business could get shut down or raided by the cops because I said something "politically incorrect" (aka: the truth) about some white person in my magazine or in an article. Yet, I'm still a hero. I ask, how many other so-called "heroes" have to think like that? Only in Amerikkka.

Just like a hoagie—a hero ain't nothin' but a sandwich. Label me a leader, not a liter. Understand? Because the ultimate goal here is to do what's right for us—not to be honored. Honor on the "Black Planet" somehow brings separation. We "heroes" have no time to bask. There's Black work to be done. But if I gotta be a sandwich, hold the mayo, the bread is already white enough for me.

WHO IZ THE MAN?
(IT DAMN-SHO
AIN'T ME)

Mo money, no money, ho money. This travels through my mind everyday as I bust my ass working, trying to make that dollar. You know, hard work and no play makes Jack a dull boy with a phat-ass pocket (that's why we call white people JACKS). Ha, sorry not me. Hard workin' Black man=lent pockets. Hell, I'm so broke my money has mayors on it instead of presidents. But still, at least once a day, without fail, I hear..."You the Man."

Who in the hell is the Man? It damn-sho ain't me. Has Black society gotten so bad that a regular brotha with employment, who just happens to make it to work four days outta the week, is considered "the Man?" What did I do to deserve this title?

As I look around my non-suburban area, I see thousands of Black folk doin' what we do best—being lazy. I also see a handful of us hustling, trying to make ends meet and somehow saving enough money to go see *Poetic Justice*, a Frankie Beverly concert, or keep our illegal cable hooked-up. As we go through our daily routine, it becomes evident that 1) ain't a damn thing changing, or 2) we ain't that special after all. Now, I prefer to believe the former, but just because my everyday struggle is a bit less than the brothas I pass on the block...does that make me "the Man?"

I'm in debt like Panama, yet brothas want to be like me. I'm getting paid $20,000 less than my white counter-parts, but "man I wish I had your job" is heard hourly. No car; brothas on the block stole, stripped, and slaved it, and still folks want to walk in my shoes (no pun intended). Bills up the WAZOO; arms are too short to box with God or Emmanuel Lewis. Thirty years old, still walkin' with my Adidas untied—stuck in P-Funk mode. What in the fk makes me "the Man?!?"

Refusing to give people money when you have it is "the Man" status. Walking slow-as-hell on your lunch hour because you aren't worried about losing your job is "the Man" status. Having control of educational, political, and industrial structures in America is definitely "the Man" status. Being able to distort minds through the control of media outlets, like television, radio, newspapers, magazines, music, and movies fits "the Man" category. Having a system that doesn't allow people to vote or come out at night is fo' real "the Man" caliber. The ability to force an entire culture to turn on itself through drugs and inward violence is crazy "the Man" status. Being able to hold a race of people down for 467 years while never losing ground in your agenda is quite frankly "the ultimate Man" status!

In my life I've been all types of niggaz. I've been the educated nigga and I've been the unemployed nigga. I've been a helluva nigga and I've also been a no-good, punk-ass, scandalous, low-down, cheap nigga. I've been the studious nigga, the drunk nigga, the basketball playin' nigga, the poor nigga, the political nigga, the blue collar nigga, the flippin' burgers nigga, the over-achieving nigga, the religious nigga, the intellectual nigga, and the almost dead nigga. The white man has allowed me to be these things, and the Black man has forced me to take pride in being all of them. Our acceptance in life has to go beyond what other people believe because some people's minds have a narrow focus. No fault of their own, but trust me—it's narrow.

If these limitations make Black folks feel that I'm "the Man"— when I have done nothing yet—then we have further to go as a culture than I ever expected. But if I'm "the Man" to them because I refuse to move out of a Black neighborhood, then cool—I'll be the Man. If I'm "the Man" because I only went to Black universities to be educated, then smoove—I be da Man. If I'm "the Man" because I've never fallen into a white woman's bed, then I am definitely the Man. If I'm "the Man" to them because I thoroughly support Black businesses, wear "X" in my heart instead of on my head, and subscribe to Emerge instead of Time, then I will die being the Man. If giving Black homeless people money to survive, but making white homeless people call me "Master" before I give them a dime makes me "the Man"...

Searchin 4 A
Ghetto Bastard

"Peace to the block, my Pops."

Tupac and Treach have a lot in common. Both are confident, young, and definitely large—not in size, but in stature. The honeys love them. And both relate to Mike Tyson—devotedly. More talented than a muthafka, both Tupac and Treach have the shit at their beck and call—like I said, they are large. Earlier this year, they both dropped hell-a-fied albums displaying skillz and anger that breed in the bodies of most young Black men. Two songs stand out on these albums because they are both centered on growing up father-less.

Now this is not a music review, this is a "life" review. Black life. Black Man Life. Most of us are okay, you know, trying to do the right thing, succeed, and stay Black at the same time. The "other" most of us (depending on whose statistics or magazines you read) don't give a fk. You know, "out there," caught up in a game bigger than we'll ever be. The fact that a large per-cent of both "most of us'" were raised without a father, makes all (not most) of us the same.

11

No one truly understands the damage of not knowing your roots. Brothas have no idea what is going on. Most of our parents are separated like siamese twins. You know what I'm sayin'—separated at birth! And I'm the one that was born.

"A ghetto bastard" is what they call me—that's what I am. Living in this cage we call the United States, I live in a society full of ghetto bastards. So yo, I ain't alone.

One of the unrecognized issues in Black manhood is the brutal impact of being raised without a father. As Black men, we grow up stuck between the bookends mentioned earlier: doing the right thing and not giving a fk. And believe me, one always outweighs the other.

Success in America don't mean shit! It doesn't bring power or respect, and if you are Black, it definitely doesn't bring peace of mind. Going through life on the solo tip, without anyone to identify with, is destructive. Everyday, everywhere, you hear Black women say, "you ain't shit and neither was your father." Now you're getting blamed for somebody else's mistake—somebody you don't even know! The hatred builds. You start hating "dude" because you're catching hell daily due to the fact that he wasn't man enough to stick around. And Momz (along with all of her sisters and sistahs) start hating you because you are starting to look more like "dude" everyday. Is this your fault? Is it mine? No. Whose ass do you kick for bringing you this grief? Nobody's. Why? 'Cause the nigger you lookin' for ain't around.

I'm so sorry. I go through life apologizing for being angry, soul searching for somebody to give me guidance. Fk that "going to the baseball park" those white boys talk about when their fathers aren't around. I got problems. I needed somebody to show me how to get a job, not push me on a swing. I needed somebody to help me deal with niggaz crazier than me, not show me how to tie a tie. I needed someone to help direct my manhood, not a role model to follow. No man has taken a vested interest in me on a daily basis. No man. Me, Tyson, Treach, Tupac, and a "whole buncha" other brothas are searching for one man in no-man's land.

Too late—I guess I'm stuck. Twenty years-old and don't give a fk. I gotta gun and no father—now who do you think got bad luck? "Daddy Was A Street Corner" and "Papa'z Song" have become my medicine. I take a dose or two a day to give my life some direction. Unable to give love, because I never received it. The only nigga in the world who can claim me has no idea who I am. I stopped asking myself "why" about three years ago. You know, why ask why? I have grown to realize that everything happens for a reason. The fellas keep tellin' me that I'll be a stronger man because of this. I say BULLSHIT! All it does is force me to come to grips with the fact that responsibility is a term my father and my people do not respect. Yet, I'm quick to call myself "Black." Ha, am I confused or what? The day will come though...

It was once said that life ain't easy. I don't think they understood exactly what that meant—because if I kill my dad when I find him, they won't blame my father, now will they?

Yo dad, holler if ya hear me.

SUPPORTING
JUNGLE FEVER:
MEET THE "G" THAT'S
KILLING ME

"**H**ell naw, kill his ass!" That's what came outta my mouth when I first saw the Spike Lee joint in 1991. That Black-on-white thang ain't happenin' and quite freddie, ('cause ain't no brothas named Frank) the brotha shoulda got taken out from the get.

Now don't get the wrong impression—like the rest of Amerikkka did—on what I'm talking about. The Black-on-white vibe I'm talking about ain't Wesley and ol' girl. I'm talking about Gator (Sam Jackson) and that rock: the destruction of the Black family by the use of crack. That's what I'm screamin' about. But just like most "negroes," too many of you looked the other way.

"Yo, that shit ain't me." That's what I said when Ted Kopple came in talking that nonsense about Blacks and crack. Every brotha ain't on crack, Ted! A community of us are "on" something, but it ain't always crack.

"Yo, Nigga loan me $10."

"Damn! I'm hit." That's what my little voice said when another friend of mine on the block caught me walking, instead of running to my car to avoid his beggin' ass. How do you refuse to take care of one of your own when his shit is through? No job, family problems, money died, landlord tossin' yo shit outta there—how do you tell the sob-story-of-life-tellin'-brotha, NO!?! You can't, 'cause it's back to the family.

Unless you've been on the shit, you will never understand what it is like. Niggas that I know who are on it—don't even want to be. That's for real. But what are you gonna do?

A lot of brothas leave doors open for other brothas to come in. Brothas you grew up with become a part of you, and by law you gotta look out for them. You know. And when the downfall starts to hit, a part of you goes down with it. There's no way to rise above it, and as a young Black man, you lose a lot very quickly. Death is third nature. Education is obsolete. And when the funerals outnumber the graduations...

But how do you deal with "self-death?" By turning your back? By not saying "no" to your boy when he wants money to "go to this job interview up north?" You merely become an around-the-way-Nino Brown/Nicky Barnes. Feeding your school-boy's habits. Tricks are for kids, right? We're both losing weight—his ass, my pockets.

Dealing in the drug game is a bitch. Sometimes I'd rather be on the inside so that I'd lose the remorse I have for brothas and sistahs who don't give a fk about themselves or their families. See, I'm family now. If ya got cash, they'll adoptyou.

"Yeah, Ma Dukes told me there'd be days like this." I never really cared because, just like the rest of Black America, I figured I was immune and the shit wouldn't affect me. My attitude was, "I'm straight and all of my people are straight. Ain't none of my niggas going out like that." WRONG!

So, of course, I wasn't prepared for the reality, and now I'm broke. Supportin' jungle fever. Too many around me are on crack. I got a family now. A family of niggas my age who depend on my well-being to keep them alive. Damn, I'm lost. Or am I just a loser? Twenty-summin' years-old, and I spend more money on hypes and *Streetwise* newspapers than I spend on my own mother. Explain the reasons. Explain life.

Something-somethang just ain't right. I ask myself is it the crack of dawn or just the dawn of crack? Do I really not understand? Do I have to be on the shit to relate? I'll probably never know. But I do understand that I'm either saving a life by supporting brothas I know on the streets, or I'm contributing to their destruction. This "Black Thang" is getting too heavy.

Ozzie Davis shot Gator at the end of that movie. My biggest problem is that he should have shot his other son.

Sugarhill

Back in March I got a card in the mail. On the front of the card was a crib. Not a baby's crib, but a phat-assed Frank Lloyd Wright-Miami Vice style crib that Black folks only see on, well...cards.

The card came from my brother—not a person off the street who happens to be my color. Instead it was from the brotha who shares my parents.

He got deep on me, asking me to remember a time when we were young, chillin', and "doin' the kids thing." Very poignantly, he sighted an incident that became very meaningful to him as we got older. Then he told me he loved me.

Two days after I received the card, I saw the movie, *Sugarhill*. Then, I realized how things in life work to make you appreciate certain nuances. After watching the movie, my brother's card meant a lot more to me; because of my brother's card, the movie meant more to me. See, this nuance shit works.

Sugarhill was a movie about brotherhood, plain and simple. The same way *The Five Heartbeats* was about friendship, *Jungle Fever* was about family, and *Forrest Gump* was about love. *Sugarhill* was about the relation-ship between two brothers who ultimately loved each other. As I watched Michael Wright go through the struggle of being a younger brother to Wesley Snipes, I watched art imitate life.

It is no family secret that my brother and I were opposites. We argued, disagreed, and kicked each other's asses when Mom wasn't doing the honors. While my brother was winning science contests, I was betting "hoodrats" that I could score 20 points on any brotha in the park. And with Pops not around, I figured my relationship with him was sometimes more father/son than brother/brother. I was sports crazy, he wasn't. I was girl crazy, he wasn't. I was money hungry, he was money appreciative. You know, two different brothas. But now that the sports don't mean as much, the "girl thang" is gone, and he makes more money than I do (smile), I've come to realize that regardless of the house on the card, and the words inside—it's the feelings that mean the most. In other words, *Sugarhill* would be Sugarshit if there was no brotherhood.

Most of the relationships shown to us as Black men are those of struggle—identity struggle. Even within our own families, we see the Black man's struggle for identity. Our brothers are often our closest enemies. Questions are raised: Who's Momma's favorite? Why does he get away with things that I don't? What's up with that allowance? It travels with us throughout our lives. The allowance competition turns into a pay check game; momma's boy turns into Momma's caretaker. We struggle to prove our manhood not only to ourselves, but to each other. But we never do it for the acceptance as much as we do it for pride, the pride that makes us who we are, the pride that makes us strong brothas. But it's also the pride that makes us stupid and brothaless.

They say every brotha ain't a brother. You know what—my problem was that I believed that.

My brother said in the card that he was sorry it took him 20 years to tell me, "Thanks." I say, I'm sorry that it took a movie to make me realize how much you mean to me.

But that's what brotherhood is all about. Loving, learning, and realizing that blood is often thicker than water, but never thicker than love. I love you back, Jack.

Now the card is on the table.

ILLUSION OF SELF

"Here you go, hold him tight," said the gynecologist the moment my life changed. The scream of my just born son made me realize that, from this moment on, I am in posession of something that I used to take for granted—a life. Got a little man to look after, another me. God bless the stress.

You never get over being a ghetto bastard. Even though I was raised in a higher stage of bastardivity, it still follows and defines me. The more the baby screamed, the more I reflected on the times I had to raise myself, answer my own questions, make my own sad choices—be fatherless. Yes, it makes a brotha much stronger, but...

Once a Black man, always a nigger. What can I do to make lil' man's life different, make him special? As a Black man, I have thousands of references to pattern my life after. But as a Black father? Nothing I've been taught, nothing I've seen, and nothing I've experienced has equipped me with the knowledge necessary to assure that my son's childhood will be better than mine. I hold my son in my hands, watching him scream, not for help, but just for notification that he's here. For the first time in my life, I feel powerless.

There is no security in being a Black man in America. Death stares you in the face the minute you are born. Black fathers disappearing like government money only makes the struggle harder. What do I do? Dr. Spock's little book can't do a damn thing for me. How do I not run out on my kid? How do I go through life and never turn my back on him? How do I not be my father to somebody else?

RIIIINNNGGG! It's Aunt Flo. She wants to know if the baby needs anything. No thank you. Love you. Click. What the baby needs is a guarantee, something not on sale at Saks or Foot Locker. There is major fear here and the Million Man March alone is not enough to help my son survive what life has in store for him.

I looked into my son's eyes on the day he came home. I asked him, "If you love me at three, just listen to me when you are 19. Please?" I knew it fell on deft ears, but I was hopeful that it would drown out all of the other subliminal messages he'll get from CNN or Montel Williams.

Then I looked at my wife, then my mother, then my aunties, god-mothers, female cousins and play sisters. I watched Nikki Giovanni and Sonja Sanchez on Bev Smith's Show, "Our Voices." I read BeBe Moore Campbell and Susan Taylor. From these women, I found strength and realization. Why do I need another brotha to teach me what I have already been taught? Through the eyes, wisdom, and guidance of the hundreds of Black women who raised me, I am now in the position to pass on a generation of learning. No Black man goes through life without receiving the necessary guidance.

The problem is that it often comes in the form of someone you ain't checking for. No Black woman will turn my child into Dennis Rodman. Everything's gonna be alright.

5AM. The wake up call. Lil' Man has no concept of time. I grab nature's blessing in the bottle and leave the room to feed him. We need to talk. Private time. I tell him things that he won't understand until he's 15. I tell him about Marcus Garvey, SNCC, Coltrane, and the Black Panther Party. I tell him about Ron Brown, Jesse Jackson Jr. and BDP. I explain to him what happened to the native Indians and why no Black man is on the money I will soon give him for allowance. I tell him this, still fearful, but with all intentions that we will wake up under the same roof the day he leaves for college. I can promise him that I will never leave him (or his mother), but I can't promise that some other brotha, another Black man, has something else in store for his life. Remember, there are no guarantees.

But it is at this time, when most other Black men are either sleep or coming home, that I build. I become Poppi, break the ghetto bastard chain. As I watch Jr. open his eyes, I see my reflection. It's an illusion of self.

A culture is only as strong as its weakest soul. From this day I must strive to never be a weak soul. I will never not wake up with my son in the morning, never make him answer his own questions, never let him raise himself.

At 9 o'clock the doorbell rings. It's Grand-Daddy. Is

he trying to make up for lost time, trying to reclaim the do wrong by doing right? The world will never know. I smile as my father takes my son in his hands. He seems proud. He asks me is there anything he can do. "Yeah," I say. "You could've asked me that question 30 years ago."

Michael, Dennis and Scottie

M. Jordan:
The Interview

Y ou guys. That's how Michael Jordan refers to you if you are in the media. It's a generalization that many of us can do without, but coming from Mike...well, you know. There's a bit of arrogance that makes us think Mike ain't talking to us when he makes the reference. Once Mike acknowledges you directly, though, everything changes. You become best friends, roots. "Mike's my man," you say to yourself. "We tight. He knows me, calls me by name. He might be talkin' to all these other chickenheads, but we go back like his old hairline. I'm special. He ain't talkin' to me."

Yeah right, wake up. Understand, Michael Jordan sees over a kazillion microphones a season. The hands and arms attached to those mics represent another world. "You guys" is as personal as it gets with Mike. And until you spend some time with him, you don't understand how lucky you are. "You guys" becomes special, an endearing term. Jordan's rules.

"You guys need me?" Michael Jordan sticks his head out of the back door in the Chicago Bull's locker room.

Nobody moves. Scottie and Dennis have everybody on lock down. Mike shrugs, "Cool." As he turns to exit, I reach out and grab his arm. "Yo Mike, who's the last person to beat you in a one-on-one?" It has been one year since he came back to the game and 14 years since he introduced himself to the world and Georgetown. He has gone the distance to prove that he's the baddest mf that's ever going to play ball. Still, there are places he won't go. This is one of them. For a man who has built his entire life on substance and meaning, trivial pursuit (dumb-ass questions) simply isn't his steelo. With a classic, no-you-didn't stop-me-for-that look, he puts my head to bed. No answer. You guys are a trip.

Two weeks later: After serving the Knicks at the Garden, Jordan steps away from the hoard of mics and lights to enter another zone. He spots my naps and gives me the nod, I follow. As we exit the locker room, leaving all the other media behind, Mike puts his arm around my shoulder and asks, "Did you get that?" "Oh yeah," I spit. "Good lookin'." Then he drops the image, "No problem Dog, anytime."

Dog. The universal term of kinship, brotha-hood...friendship. Me and Mike. No mo' Mars. As Patrick Ewing and Charles Oakley push me aside for more pressing conversation, I give Mike a pound, he gives me the wink. What else are friends for? Oh, by the way, this is what Money gave his "Dog."

SLAM: Your love for basketball. How deep is it?
MIKE: "My love for the game is very deep right now. It's as deep as it has ever been. That's why I came back last year. I enjoyed baseball after I retired, but basketball

gives me something more. I have never enjoyed a season as much as the one we are having right now. Scottie has matured and the team has really gelled. The guys on this team really get along, there is no jealously or animosity. We just play ball, win, and have fun."

SLAM: Are you in a groove?
JORDAN: "I don't know, you tell me. I feel very comfortable. I feel in control of my game. I feel like I'm right back at the same level that I was at before I retired, maybe in some ways better mentally. I worked real hard to get back to where I am."

SLAM: But I mean, right now you're rollin'. Your game is on-on, you know what I'm sayin'? What's it feel like when you get in one of these grooves? What goes through your mind?
MONEY: "To keep it goin', you know. Just try to find certain rhythms, certain tendencies throughout the course of a game — throughout the course of the day— that maintains so that it continues. That's important."

SLAM: Is that hard?
GOD: "Yeah it's hard. Especially if everybody doesn't take it the same way, or take the seriousness of it every single night. I mean, I joke and I kid around, but once I step in between those lines I like to maintain the same attitude I had the game before, you know?"

SLAM: Ok, lets go back (you know how we do). The game of basketball itself is one of culture. As a brotha who's considered the essence of the culture, explain to me what you feel the importance of street ball is to the total game and what it represents?

BLACK JESUS: "I think playing basketball on the street is what the game should be about. Especially for the youngsters. I will encourage my kids to go out with their friends to the playgrounds, get a game, and play. For as long as they want. You develop friendships, competition, and teamwork on the playground. I can't imagine a better way to spend time."

SLAM: Were you a playground legend?

MJ: (Giving up that look again) "Next... "

SLAM: So are pick-up games still important to you? I mean, I heard your brother Larry used to...

AIR: "Man, my older brother Larry used to kill me! He was older and bigger than me. He would beat me, talk to me, and not let me forget about it. What that did for me was make me work that much harder to beat him. He had no idea that I was going to end up taller than him. I look at my games with him as a great experience when I was young because I developed my love for the game, and it made me work harder to get better."

SLAM: So besides Larry, who is the best ball player that you've ever played against that we've never heard of?

THE MAN: (The look again) "Next... "

SLAM: A'ight, one by one how did the old school influence your game? Elgin Baylor, Julius Erving, David Thompson, Connie Hawkins... How did they influence your game?

JORDAN: "I was different. Growing up in North Carolina I wasn't exposed to basketball nationally—I just followed North Carolina and wanted to go there. I used to watch David Thompson and Walter Davis. Then when I met and talked to (Coach) Dean Smith, I knew..."

SLAM: You knew what?
$: " I knew (UNC) was the place for me."

SLAM: What means the most to you right now?
$: "Right now?"

SLAM: Right now.
$: "Simple, staying healthy and winning another championship."

SLAM: It's crunch time now, aren't you getting tired? I mean, this is your first full season back in a couple. Wassup? You're making it hard for Phil to give you some rest.
MIKE: "You should know me by now, I haven't changed. This is the most challenging part of the season and I thrive on it, on this type of competitiveness. I just try to elevate my game and everyone else's game surrounding me. To some degree, that's the type of thing I thrive on, I enjoy it. I want to make it tough for Phil to take me out, because I enjoy playing in these types of circumstances. Hey Dog, I'm getting old and I may not get these thrills too often anymore (smile)."

SLAM: 70
MICHAEL: "It was not a goal. It was not something we started out the season to achieve, but when it got within reach we wanted to do it. Don't forget we didn't start out the season saying we were going to win 70 games.

We started out the season saying we're going to win a championship. This team has a lot of confidence. We have a good rhythm to the way we play. We believe we can win every game we step on the court to play. We know how to focus on games, especially when we didn't do well the game before."

SLAM: Like that 20 point loss to the Knicks...
No.23: "Next..."

In the first game of the season, James Caffey got nervous. As a rookie, he felt that the Bulls were losing to Charlotte at half-time because of him. Never pressed, Mike pulled him to the side and taught. "I told him," Jordan says, "just play the game of basketball. It's simple. If you can't remember the plays, it's cool. Don't worry about it. Just do the things that got you here. Set a screen, get a rebound. Just play ball."

Caffey didn't play much better in the second half, but Mike did. He took his own advice and simply came out and played ball. The way only he knows how. Lead by example. Move as a team, never move alone. Yo son, just do it.

It's difficult to stay motivated when nobody can fk with you. But Jordan still finds challenges. At times, even he doesn't feel like he's the best in the game. It's not his humility or humbleness, it's his honesty. Despite everything, Jordan still feels that there's a lot of James Caffey left in him. There's still alot to learn, there's still room for improvement. The only difference between him and Caffey is experience. The game of basketball tells him this every night, and he does more than listen; he pays attention and builds. Life, to Jordan, is not a game, but basketball is life. As he goes, so does the game. But he'll be the first to tell you that it's never all about him.

SLAM: You still get motivated?
MJ: "Each time I step on the basketball court. I have a motivation to either prove something to myself or to prove something to you or to the other team. I don't like to lose. This team doesn't like to lose. That's motivation within itself. It's a definite and a don't. Either way, you don't want to lose and that's the motivation."

SLAM: Game situation: score tied in the fourth. What do you personally put on yourself in those situations?
MJ: "It's just a matter of buckling down and making some big plays. Usually, I can get a team ignited and pull off a stretch (run). It's important to get that first burst of energy before the other team does, because if they get it before you do they'll get more confidence— and that's the one thing you don't want to happen."

SLAM: OK, no more game q's. If you only had $5, who would you pay to see play ball?
MJ: "I would pay to see Scottie Pippen play. I think he is the ultimate team player. A guy that can score, pass, rebound, and play defense. I also think he's great to have in the locker room. We have been closer this year, and I have really enjoyed that."

SLAM: I heard through the grapevine that you and Scottie have never played each other in a one-on-one. Drop the diplomacy, what would happen if you two went at it?

MJ: "I honestly don't know. I don't know what would happen, but there'd be a lot of talkin' going on. Sometimes we are on opposite teams in practice and go at each other. That's always fun, but my team usually wins."

SLAM: As a fan of basketball, what has been your biggest thrill? In other words, outside of your personal accomplishments, what has given you the greatest joy? What has made you smile the most?
MJ: "One of the things I can say that I enjoy the most is watching my teammates grow and become part of something special. Guys like Randy Brown, Steve Kerr, Luc Longley, Bill Winnington, and Ron Harper—they have never been a part of a championship-type team like we have right now. Now that they have a chance, I want them to enjoy it because they know how hard it is to get there. But we haven't gotten there yet. I just have to make sure I do what I have to do so that we can get there."

SLAM: What's the biggest difference in you since you came back? Besides that turn around jumper.
MJ: (Laugh) "I think I've matured. I'm in more control of my personal life, as well as my basketball life. I went and took a break from 'you guys'. I think my last two years away made me mature enough to deal with a lot of things surrounding my life in general. I'm just in better control of myself right now. I'm glad to be back. And I think I deserve to come back and play the game I truly love."

SLAM: Are you that good?
MJ: "I'm alright."

SLAM: Have you ever seen anybody do anything on the court that made you say, "Damn, I wish I could do that?"

MJ: " I'm telling you, Scottie does a lot of things on the court that amaze me. He moves really well and has those long arms and legs, and basically has no weakness. Also, he has matured and is confident of his role on this team. At times, he amazes me."

SLAM: Dog, there's one question I've always wanted to ask you...when you see other players wearing Air Jordans—your shoes—what do you say to 'em?

MJ: "I tell them, 'Don't embarrass my shoes'."

SLAM: You say that to everybody?

MJ: "Everybody that wears 'em."

SLAM: Anything else you'd like to say?

MJ: "Yeah, for all those people who say that I lost a step, I think I've proven that there are other ways to make that step (smile)."

SLAM: Yo Dog, wassup with the new contract next year...

MJ: "Next..."

THE NIGGA U LOVE 2 HATE / DENNIS II SOCIETY

Step into his world, exit quickly. Get your hair colored and your fingernails painted. Spend a few paychecks on tatoos and body piercing. Grab 20 rebounds, stop Shaq from scoring in crunchtime, get dressed, and leave.

"I came here to kick some ass. That's all. I don't smile or laugh. Call me Satan. On the court, I go out there and do my job for the people in Chicago and this team. People come to see the Bulls win and if I'm not out there doing the job, then I need to get the hell up outta here."

Number 91. There's only one in the world. Dennis Rodman is to the NBA what Howard Stern is to the FCC, Dennis II Society. He is unquestionably the best rebounder in basketball and—when he puts his mind to it—the best defensive player in professional sports. He has an unreal talent and a relentlessness to win that destroys opposing teams. Broken down: You'd rather have this muthafucka on your squad than have to play against him.

He's the last brotha you want to see in an alley at night or in your bed the next morning, and he damn sure ain't the brotha you want to go up against if you're a power forward in the NBA. He's a brotha from another planet. In defining Dennis Rodman, basketball is often a subplot. He rocked the MTV Awards with his EnVogue tank top and Barbara Eden's genie drawers, screaming to the world, "I just felt a little gay tonight."

Yet, this is the same brotha that scared the white off Santa (and his elves) in last year's Nike TV spot, making demands that would have made every member of the Junior M.A.F.I.A. proud. He launched his own magazine and has an autobiography on the shelf called, *Bad As I Wanna Be.* Too live. He's the whitest Black man in the country next to OJ. He parties on like Wayne and Garth, rides a Harley, loves Pearl Jam, and hangs with Jack Daniels, oh I'm sorry, Jack Haley. The only "Black thing" Dennis has done in the last five years is sleep with Madonna...and now she's bitchin'.

He is misunderstood because he lives life on his own terms, but Rodman's not looking for understanding. He wants respect. His resume shows he is an NBA All-Star with three NBA championship rings, five rebounding titles, and two defensive player-of-the-year awards. Neither Jordan or Pippen, nor Shaq or Penny can claim that.

As he walks through the Bull's practice facility, he stares deeply at something. Reporters surround him, never understanding his focus. Questions and answers, questions and answers. He fields 'em like Kim, living single in the game of basketball that pays his rent, but a game he could give less than a fk about.

In walks Michael Jordan. Nobody moves, nobody notices. The green-haired bandit has snatched the "lime" light. Michael loves it; Dennis doesn't really care. His focus is elsewhere, but don't go there—you might come out scared.

"I don't think I'm going to be remembered as one of the greatest basketball players ever," Rodman says as he watches GOD 23 leave the building. "I'll be remembered as the wildest, craziest tattooed guy in the world. Ain't no way in hell people are going to remember Dennis Rodman ten years from now. That's what I want. I want there to be a misconception about me. People love to hate me. I don't give a damn about people that hate me. I just want to be allowed to be me. They say I'm dumb, stupid, and uncoachable. (One day) they're going to realize that Dennis Rodman's a lot smarter than anyone thinks."

His addition to the Bulls turned them from potential Eastern conference challengers to the greatest team ever. Rodman brought the pain and the tenacity needed to push the Bulls to the next level. The team had been in desperate need to fill the void left by Horace Grant when he stepped to Magic city. Now, just in the Nick of time, the Bulls got the one man who can play "D" on Horace Grant, Nick Anderson, or anybody on the Seattle Supersonics.

"On paper, this could be our best team ever," Jordan said. "The challenge for us is to gel as a team. Dennis? He brings a lot to the table. He's been playing against this offense so long he probably knows it better than some of us."

But, yo Mike, have you ever played with somebody that lives with his own hairdresser?

"You don't want me to answer that."

No joke, give it up.

"No," holding back crazy laughter, "I haven't."

The Difference. That should be Rodman's nickname. It describes him best and on all levels. He's different than the average brotha, and he makes a difference on the court and in the outcome of games. He easily has the best I-don't-give-a-fk attitude in sports. He can irritate the world and, at the same time, make Scottie Pippen play better.

"Don't go there," Pippen requests. "Look, I hated the guy when I competed against him. I don't think I'll ever forget (some of the things Rodman did, like pushing Pippen into the basket post, cutting open his chin in a 1991 playoff game when Rodman was with the Bad Boys in Detroit). But, I realize now that we are teammates, and we're going to have to get along on the court. Off the court? There's not going to be any love between us. I haven't had a conversation with him. Probably never will." But, for some reason, Pip has a new unseen fire in his game that has many (even some magazines) calling him the best basketball player in the world. Wonder where that came from?

"I didn't come here to make friends," Rodman opens. "I used to slam Jordan and Pippen in Detroit, what the hell. This is just basketball. It's my job to play basketball. As far as a relationship with Michael and Scottie...I don't sleep with them. I don't sleep with Michael. I don't sleep with Scottie. If I did, I'd use a condom. Safe sex. But I'm not here for Michael or Scottie. I'm here to work my ass off and help the Chicago Bulls, and give them a championship."

Fk being hard, Dennis Rodman is complicated. As the NBA season goes, so does the "Worm." He's the new nigga on the block in a city that "don't like" niggas, but loves niggers. Dennis is perfect for this crime, stealing an NBA crown in Al Capone's ill-segregated town. His attitude and behavior increases his white fan base, while his defiance and color gets him love from the brothas. His ability to rebound, defend, and create fast breaks with uncanny outlet passes, plus his work ethic, makes him colorless and just a helluva ball player. But he doesn't care, he can give less than a fk. That's the beauty of it. That's the difference.

"Some people wish they could be in my shoes. Hey, if this doesn't work out, if nothing goes right in Chicago, I'll just graze the grass like a horse. Live off $10 a day. It doesn't matter to me. Too many guys come into this league worried about (the wrong thing). They don't give a damn about basketball's Alonzo Mourning, saying no to $10 million a year! You tell me, is he worried about the game of basketball?

"I take pride in kickin' somebody's ass on the basketball court, then shaking his hand and saying, 'You had a nice game.' It's the determination and the strength and the power to go and get the basketball. People are wondering, 'How in the hell is he doing it?' I'm only 215, 6'6" and I'm getting 16-something rebounds a game. C'mon! Like I said, one day they're going to realize Dennis Rodman's a lot smarter than anyone thinks, and when that day comes, I'll be gone."

Then he sneaks back into the realism..."Isn't it amazing how many guys in the NBA have tattoos now? I wonder where they're getting that from?"

THE LEGEND OF AFROMAN

"Hey kid, we need you to do us a favor. Uh, we know this is short notice, but, uh, we need you to fill in for Superman. See, out of the blue, he (Superman) quit, retired, uh, changed sports. Now, uh, we need you to do his job. We can't pay you any extra money, there are other players we have to cater to right now, but we'd really, really appreciate it if you could score more points, play more minutes, grab more rebounds, dish out more assists, and lead us back to the NBA Finals for our fourth championship in a row. Now we realize this is an impossible task, but, uh, we have no choice. Can you help us?"

-J. Krause?

Most athletes have one defining moment in their careers that either glorifies them or that haunts them forever. Mike Tyson will always have to explain (among other things) his loss to Buster Douglas. Roberto Duran will never outlive his "no mas" experience. Bill Buckner has his New York Mets' moment, and we all know Craig Elo's.

Scottie Pippen, unfortunately, has a few. It took

him years to live down his migraine against the Pistons in 1988, and just when people forgot about that, BAM, Scottie decides to take the most expensive, most publicized, and most well-deserved chill in sports history. And that was just the beginning.

Being "The One" is never easy. All superheroes carry the world, or some franchise, on their shoulders—taking all losses in stride and smiling at every child who demands an autograph or a role model lesson 'cause Pops ain't acting right.

Over the past ten years, Chicago has had the honor of hosting the AirGod Show. After three championships, Michael Jordan cancelled his show and ended the most impressive display of superheroism witnessed since Forrest Gump taught Elvis how to dance. America was in need of a David Robinson? Too clean. Shaquille O'Neal? Too big. The only person in the position to "replace" Jordan was the man who shared a fraction of the spotlight with him, his partner, his side-kick, his Kato.

In October 1993, Scottie Pippen became that man. Never asking for the honor, he stood in the corner of Jordan's retirement press conference wearing dark glasses and looking into an even darker future. At that moment, he became the replacement, the new superhero, the ONE.

Enter AFROMAN, superbrotha of the 90's, superfly like the 70's. Even before he grew the puffed dome, Scottie Pippen asserted himself as the ball player who was faster than a speeding bullet, more powerful than the Bulls front office, and able to leap tall Ewing's in a single bound...he was on that tip. Even beyond his own beliefs, Pip brought the Bulls within one win of the previous year's regular season record (a squad that included MJ) and one foul away from championship number four (because honestly neither Indiana nor Houston coulda hung if...). He won the NBA All-Star game MVP, and damn-near snagged the award for the entire season last year. He was asked to replace "god" on the spot, with no immediate warning—and he did it! Nuff respect? No respect.

Every superhero has obstacles. In Pip's case they can be called roadblocks. He was stopped by Chicago's finest for carrying a legally registered gun in his car—obstacle one. He called Chicago fans "racist" for booing him and other Black players—obstacle two. Then, the Bull's "mis-management" ignored Pip's demand for mo' money. Instead, they flew to Europe and offered mad money to an un-proven rookie, Pip's future replacement—ROADBLOCK.

Pippen had to go through last season looking in the mirror everyday, knowing that someone from Europe named Kukoc (along with forty other NBA players) was making more money than him.

"I look at the games as a whole," Pip said one evening while discussing his stock in the NBA. "I see a lot of players that are great players. Olajuwon, David (Robinson), Larry Johnson—those are the type of guys that stick out in my mind as some of the top players in the league. I feel complimented when people tell me that (I'm one of the best), but it's hard to think that way when they're not paying you that way."

As a man, how do you deal with this? As a superhero, how do you justify swallowing your pride and honor for a lucky number 7, the latest great white hope? Would Larry Bird have sat and watched the Celtics do the same thing to him with M.L. Carr? Hell no. But in the eyes of the American sports fan, Pippen was trippin'. Then came game three against the Knicks.

When Pip decided to "relax," and not play in that final 1.8 seconds, he disobeyed every rule ever applied to practical obedience and protocol. Finally, super-nig had gone crazy. "No team player would ever do that!!!" they cried. An entire city went into an uproar. Scottie was over. He chilled in that chair listening to Bill Cartwright bitch and watched Chicago's great white hope hit the winning basket. Void of kryptonite, Scottie Pippen had done the unheard of for any superhero: He looked out for Scottie Pippen.

One day before a game, I asked Afroman why he couldn't argue with me about being the best in the league, he replied with a laugh, "'Cause you're telling the truth." Pound for pound, Scottie Pippen is the best player in the NBA—just ask Michael Jordan. Controversial and outspoken, Pip has endured more scrutiny than Ted Kennedy and put up with more "fables" than Aesop. Mad, humble Southern beginnings and untapped hoop skills brought him into the NBA as an unknown, but he watched and he learned. During those early years, many questioned his heart. Haunted by a headache in Detroit and a McDaniels in New York, his life changed dramatically when the Bulls coach, Phil Jackson, decided to "let" him guard Magic Johnson in game two of the 1990 NBA Finals. Shazzammm! The team never lost another game in that series, and Pip was finally the man playin' next to the man.

When he made Dream Team I, his stock went ballistic. "It was a dream come true," he said. This league— well, the coaches in the league—acknowledged his worth along with his talent. His play even propelled Julius Erving (the original superhero) to call Scottie "the best 2-man in the history of the game." Sorry John Stockton, Pip's the shit!

"I'm a big fan of Scottie's and I've known him for awhile," says Bulls guard/forward, Pete Myers. "But what (he's) doing now is unbelievable to me and he's not getting the credit he deserves. Look at ESPN or CNN every night, they're not paying much attention to him. I don't think there is any question who is the best forward and one of the best two or three players in the league—it's Scottie Pippen."

"Yo Harp, handicap H-O-R-S-E, you shoot first," Pip says to teammate Ron Harper with a smile after an intense practice session that has every player dripping. Relaxed and confident, even in a game of H-O-R-S-E, Scottie uses his skills to take advantage of other players' weaknesses.

"His shit ain't got no form! Look at it. A'ight Harp, left hand dunk off one foot."

"Naw, I said no dunkin'," Harper replies.

Scottie laughs, "Left hand three off glass then."

The bank is open, Harp is outta there and Scottie gets serious. His left hand is not a handicap, it's his greatest asset. He stays on the court an extra 20 minutes working on his left hand. He hasn't worked on it in a while, but it still looks sweet. From hook shot to finger rolls, Scottie plays a one-on-one with himself, determined to find a comfort zone for his rhythmic left. He smiles only when he feels the groove. "It's coming back," he whispers as his teammates rush to the weight rooms and showers that precede their exit from the gym.

Michael Jordan once said that the only thing he

couldn't do that Scottie could was drive to the hole and dunk on people with his left hand. Michael's not alone. There are about 200 other players in the league who feel the same way and have fallen victim to the same pain. Pip's left hand, and his ability to use it to bring embarrassment to others, is what truly separates him from NBA mortals. He uses it to lead the league in triple-doubles and steals. He uses it to nullify weak shit that comes down the lane and to collect the hundreds of bricks that attack backboards and rims in stadiums across the country. He uses it to pound on his chest when his other hand is at work slammin', shootin', dribblin', thievin', and boardin' against all the NBA bad guys who try to dethrone his city. Night in and night out, he uses his left to play the type of basketball that reminds us of Dr. J and The Iceman back in the ABA days. Smooth, unique, and at times, unstoppable. The superhero uses his weapon well because his city has left him no other choice.

Left alone to fly solo, Pip is doin' his thang. Remember, Pippen ain't easy. Rightfully ripping the "snake-management" apart, calling a spade a spade and a liar "a liar" whenever he feels the need, yet playing to a level that only Hakeem could match. He wears his uniform as a badge of honor. Through all of the madness, he prevails and proves "beyond any reasonable doubt" (OJ court case language) that he deserves to be respected and revered as a franchise player—one of the league's best—the one keeping the arena filled.

As the forces around him close in, he screams for an exit. "At this stage of my career, I've done a lot for the team and the organization. If I'm deserving of the treatment I'm getting, someone tell me why. If not, get me out of here." He's down to number four on the Bulls payroll. BJ Armstrong, Ron Harper, and Tony Kukoc can afford to buy him lunch.

The media claims he has a beef with Kukoc. Absurd. During shoot-arounds they play "soccer" together and off-the-court they battle one another at video games. They're cool. They may not be the best of friends but, then, neither are David Stern and Bill Murray. Pippen just wants more appreciation for the work that he has done.

"(For $8 million a year) I still don't think I'd be happy here. This is because of the bridges that have been burned by my being here," Pip inhales, releases, and then continues. "Them trying to trade me and things like that. My hard work and work ethic aren't enough. That shows right there that I'm not appreciated." Other players around the league ask for it, some even receive it. Not here, the situation is too far gone and there's no way back.

"I have to side with Scottie," says a never-to-be-named Bulls player in a *Chicago Sun-Times* interview, "but I don't want my name used because I've had my own problems with (them). The only question is how long can a player who knows better choose to put up with a certain mess. Some guys can't holler as loud as others, so we have to put up with some lying or whatever else, or we'll have to go to Europe or the CBA."

In the words of All-Star forward Horace Grant: "I spent seven years (there) with an organization I didn't care much for." Flagrant foul, Rodman style.

In addition to having to deal with the Bulls "ill-management," Pippen has to put up with attacks on his character. Sam Smith, for instance, of the *Chicago Tribune* calls Pippen, "stubborn...(which) leads to some of his astonishing behavior." Smith needs to follow baseball and hockey, there he will see some "astonishing behavior."

Afroman, so unappreciated. Although Pippen was the soul (and heart) of the team last year, the Bulls "diss-management" up-graded Kukoc's contract to $26 million over six years, and tried to send Pippen elsewhere. "No-management" denies it, but Seattle knows it, Kemp knows it, and Scottie damn sure knows it. The $9.6 million Scottie has to "live" with over the next four years is minimum wage in this league. A slap in the face to a superhero.

Christmas night 1994, Afroman had to throw his cape back on. The Bulls annual meeting with the Knicks needed to be saved. With his coach complaining that he does "too much", Pip played all 53 minutes of the game—and HAD to score all of the team's points in overtime to secure a victory. The numbers were average: 36 points, 16 rebounds, two blocked shots in the last three seconds, you know the inside stuff. "Thanks Afroman, you saved us from embarrassment once again." Can anybody say, "We love you Afroman?" Didn't think so.

Back in the lab, the NBA has always, and will always continue to serve as a breeding ground for today's superheroes. Yeah, Deion is going to get his, but shorties from block to block spend hours on the asphalt bassin' defenders left and right, imitating what they feel is real and calling out the superstars' names as they go along:

"Kemp."

"Penny."

"Zo, on that ass."

"Starks for threeeeee..."

"Oh snap, you just got shook Kenny A. style."

"Killa crossover, Timmy baby! C-Ya!"

"Pippen, mutha..." PIPPEN? Stop the game.

"Hold up, kid. He ain't the man."

"Yeah, Grant Hill's the man!"

"Plus that afro is wack and he ain't gettin' paid!" Game resumes.

"Kukoc!"

"Down low, ahh. Big Dog fool."

"Like LJ, I'm too much man for you down here. Bacdafkup son."

"Oooh, that was some old school Jordan-type shit..."

With the fist-sculptured pic in his hair, Afroman moves on. Who knows where he'll wind up. For now, it's good enough to survive. Afroman's alter ego is too cool to let the b.s. get to him forever. So he tosses a few chairs, they're lucky he doesn't have Colin Ferguson's morals.

"I have to put my words in and let them know how I feel," he diplomatically told NBC. "Do I want to get anything off of my chest?..."

We both laugh, realizing that His Afroness may never get the props or the bank he deserves. He has to keep reminding himself, time and time again, that this is America, a place where superheroes, not superstars, always work for free.

Jordan: *Slam*, May 1996; Scottie: *Slam*, January 1996; Rodman: *The Source*, February 1996

Dead Poet Society

ABITCHIZABITCH

The GOP's Contract with Hiphop

A female dog or a problem? Whoever thought up the word "bitch" did not know there were so many areas that could be covered in five letters. Sorry to inform you, but this is not about disrespecting Black women or punk, scared, sissy-ass negroes...this is about life. Real life. This is the "real" deal that niggas are too scared to face, the shit we run from. Like bitches.

The alliance in hiphop has never really been political. Yes, there have been some Black brothas talkin' that "Black shit" and droppin' fluid on the mic, but ain't nobody run for office. Last year the white boys network (WBN) got back control of the world when the Republican Party successfully invaded Congress. That "take over" of an already Limbaughish Congress means: our Black "thang" is over. Turn off the lights and get your Martin Lawrence watchin'-ass out. It's time to listen to what Souljah told us four years ago: Slavery is back in effect.

Cypress Hill. Capitol Hill. They have Newt, we got Snoop. He calls the president's wife a bitch, Snoop calls your daughter the same. What's the big deal? A bitch is one regardless of gender, expression, or social beliefs. It's a bitch to think that, for the next 40 years, upscale, uptight, Republican, whiter-than-white Americans are going to control the country, like the liberal, Democratic, white ones weren't bad enough.

It's a bitch to think that affirmative action laws, social reforms, and amendments we have used to gain leverage in this Cell Block H of a country are about to be "abolished" (slave talk). It's a bitch to think that over the next six years, $10.5 billion will be spent on building, expanding, and operating prisons (which will no doubt increase the prison population—and everybody knows what that means) instead of using that money to assist community service programs, secure financial assistance for educational systems, or to provide employment and training opportunities for the 80 kazillion Black folks for whom they're building the prisons. Who's the bitch now?

The culture of hiphop has never embraced a political agenda. After 20 years of singing songs without solutions, we are now forced to swallow our own rhetoric, our own bullshit. The time has come for those so-called players, pimps, gangstas, and hard rhymin' heads to get off Biggie's zipper and find out who Bob Dole is. What effect is the "Contract With America" going to have on our lives?

Yeah, Gingrich and tonic, Gin and juice. The new flavors of the month. Sip the juice, there is enough to go around. Everybody drinking and having a good time, and missing the point. This is real gangstaism:
* Allowing states to deny aid to mothers younger than 18.
* Allowing states to decide if welfare recipients must

work to receive benefits.
 * Changing the income tax code.
 * Setting new term limits for members of Congress.
 * No tax breaks for 48% of the families earning less than
$200,000 a year.
 *Eliminating congressional spending for informal
groups like the Congressional Black Caucus.

Give 'em five on the white handside. The new
Congress will be the KKK in three-piece suits. Sears and
JC Penny will have "white" sales every other day; the
sheets are going to be in demand. But the majority of the
hiphop crowd is unfazed, too concerned about beats
and rhyme flow. How lost can one nation be?
 In the struggle to save our "Black" souls, this may
be a blessing in drag. Instead of waitin' for hand-outs,
aid checks, and free rides, maybe this is what's needed
to really "move the crowd." That Black Planet everybody was in love with five years ago may now have a
real reason to exist. Remember, Amerikkka's new political reform has targeted us.
 The reality of the Republican agenda is about to
slap hiphop in the face. This is exactly what is needed.
Young Black America is embedded in a musical culture
that has lost direction, focus, and the desire to take on
anything bigger than MTV. Lyrical knowledge has to
return to its creative home. KRS can't continue to save
us all of the time. He needs help. Edutainment, what's
that all about?
 The next revolution will be televised, therefore
Black folks won't miss it. Congress' "newt" committ-
ment: cut $1.4 trillion. Who do you think is going to feel
that first? On the day he took office as the new Speaker

Of The House (becoming the second most powerful person in the world; the one he calls "bitch," Hillary, is the first), Newt Gingrich said, "This is a moral crisis equal to segregation, equal to slavery. We owe it to our children and grandchildren to get this government in order." Republican style. Ain't that a bitch.

FUTURE SHOCK 1996:
The Nationalistic Ballistics

For the next few minutes call me Stephen King—Rodney King's little brother—cause I came here to scare some people...white people. Back in the day, there was a play entitled "A Day Of Absence." In this play, Black people collectively decided to remove themselves from society for a day—no school, no work, no nothing. Black folks removed themselves from "the system"—and would not tell white people why. White people snapped! They swore the "negroes" were plotting a massive take-over and were about to pay them back for everything they'd done to them. Guilt set in and fear turned into paranoia, and the rest is history...

Enter rap music. There is a thin line that divides insanity and genius. For years the credibility of rap has been tested. It has been called everything from the cause of social destruction to the "most brain-dead pop music" ever heard. At the same time, rap has opened America's eyes to Afrocentricity, helped Nelson Mandela survive, and attracted the attention of presidential candidates and law enforcement officals.

The duality of rap's responsibility to entertain and to educate has come full circle. Young Black minds have taken political stands and have addressed issues of concern to Black American culture. As Chuck D. always says, "Rap is Black America's CNN," but it ain't our Jesse Jackson.

The theory I bring is one of promise, one of fear, and one of solidarity. Considering rap's influence upon the public, rap's concern for the Black community, and Black America's total lack of political power, what would happen if a member of the hiphop community ran for President of the United States. Think about it, white American could be facing its worst nightmare—a real nigga in the Oval Office.

It might be our only hope. Jesse can't do it; Colin ain't gonna do it. We have over 200 powerless Black mayors across the country, no governors, one senator, and a host of Black bureacrats, from Clarence Thomas to Vernon Jordan, who are blind to Black reality. Rap's all we got left. They are the only ones who show concern for all Black Americans, not just the middle class.

Ice Cube for President! Sound strange? Well, let's do this: establish a ticket that has Sister Souljah as Vice President; KRS-One as Secretary of Education; Q-Tip as Secretary of State; Professor Griff as Chief of Staff; Kool Moe Dee, Heavy D., and Doug E. Fresh as drug czars; Chuck D. as Commissioner of the FCC; Queen Latifah as Secretary of Housing and Urban Development; and Ice T as Secretary of Defense.

Who would vote for this ticket? Well, the millions of people who pushed the combined sales of these artist to over 125 million records sold. The money and support to run the campaign could come from the artist's personal investments, other members of the rap community (including Russell Simmons and Sean "Puffy" Combs), other Black artists and entrepreneurs (including Spike Lee, Quincy Jones, Eddie Murphy, Johnnie Cochran, and Bob Johnson), community, civic and legislative leaders (including Al Sharpton, Mike McGee, Maxine Waters, and Charles Rangle), sports figures (including Jim Brown, Magic Johnson, Deion Sanders, Tiger Woods, and Michael Jordan), members of the Congressional Black Caucus, the NAACP, and other individual contributors.

Politics is a numbers game. Reach one, teach some; One man, some votes. Regardless of what ideas a candidate has, or what issues he or she addresses—without votes there is no movement. Rap artists, positive or negative, have the largest following of any collection of Black individuals in America. Members of the hiphop nation can bring political awareness to young African Americans, dismantle the apathetic nature of African Americans, and eliminate the thought that "if God had wanted us (Black people) to vote, He would have given us candidates."

White America's biggest fear has been either a Black man with a gun, or a Black man with a following. Too many Black men have guns and are doing the wrong things with them. Any Black leader with a following who has stood up for civil rights has been shut down. Amerikkka has always found a way to put a limit on the powerful Black individual. African Americans need a force of individuals who share the same mindset toward the national and global betterment of Black people. We need a movement, not a move man!

Will whites who buy rap records support this ticet? Naaahh. They may have pictures of Michael Jordan and Shaq on the bedroom wall; Oprah and Colin Powell on the living-room mantel; and Wesley Snipes and Heather Hunter hidden in their underwear drawer, but...

Hiphop has shown that, as an idiom, it can sustain the scrutiny and media racialization placed on all Blacks living in Amerikkka. It has invited the apprehensive and non-apprehensive African American to "party for your right to fight." It has brought about change, sparked political awareness, and challenged every symbol representative of the American mainstream. Though inconsistent in certain areas, rap has been the spokesperson for the Black cause worldwide.

Hiphop has filled every qualification needed to politically represent Black people, without being qualified. This is something to think about, something to cherish, something to be afraid of. The new Black Power movement is not going to be like the one that moved us 30 years ago. The new movement is fully aware of the mistakes made and the opportunities missed during the Sixties. They refuse to let it happen again.

Ice Cube's fictitious run for presidency could be something America has to take seriously. Whether the outcome is victorious or not—credibility will come from this campaign. From credibility comes power—political power! This can be the same type of power that got Reagan, an actor, into office. Black America needs an Ice Cube for President and a Sister Souljah for Vice President. Think about it.

BORN CRIMINAL BORN

Everybody loves a rags to riches story, but nobody likes to hear a true one—at least not when it involves an American brotha or sistah. Over the decades, Black has become synonymous with underachievement, crime, ignorance, and substance abuse. This, of course, is a white thing. Today, thousands of individuals (Black and white) deal in "illicit activity" to get the bills paid.

Lately, the rap community has been under siege because of it's "glorification of drug use." "The drug game," said one record company executive, "is just as big a part of rap music as gold chains." Whoa! Is this line of thinking outdated, incorrect, or just blatantly racist? Probably all three. Yes, some rap artists have histories of drug involvement, but not nearly enough to place an entire stereotype on a culture. Hell, this ain't rock n' roll.

Ice T, Ice Cube, KRS-One, Grand Puba, Heavy D, and Q-Tip have all said that they have "at least smoked weed" once in awhile. A few have sold "bud" to keep ends in their pockets. The New York God, Rakim, has endured allegations concerning his selling weight. Yeah, they try to get us. The Beastie Boys have made three albums talking about "gettin' fk'ed up" and it's cool, but the minute BIGGIE talks about how he used to sell shit—stories begin appearing about rap and a billion dollar-a-month drug industry, and Slick Rick is targeted and jailed for less-than-a-$100 substance incident? Who's the real criminal?

The role that drugs and alcohol play in the African American community, unfortunately enough, is large. Many Black people are dependent upon one substance or another for some means of escape. Either we try to escape our psychological situation by doing drugs, or we try to escape our economic situation by selling drugs. Many rap artists are simply products of the hood, born into an arena of economic depression. One of the opportunities offered to us, as Blacks, is "selling substances" in order to climb the caging fence. Rap artists who once used "the trade" as a means to an end, are now some of corporate America's economic equals. Legally! This is what bothers white society (Born Criminals) about Black folk (Learned Criminals). To them, it is horrifying for a young Black ex-"drug- dealing, Uzi-toting nigga of rap music" to be an American icon. But it's cool for Tim "I was once a convict for dealing cocaine" Allen to have a Top 10 television show (Home Improvement) and host the 1992 Emmy Awards. Now, can you say Kelsey Grammer? Go Figure.

Substance use in minority communities is not indicative of substance use in the Hiphop community. Rap artists can not be exploited or played against the grain when it comes to capitalism in America. That is too hypocritical. They have turned bad into good, shit into sugar, rags into riches. The fact that many of these artists are "ex" drug whatevers should be a testament to their inner strength. So without further ado, let's drop this association because it's old, as well as racist. Hey, if Bill Clinton was forgiven for (Ha!) "inhaling," then the rest of the rap community must be forgiven for selling anything other than records.

Living in A Balakunphution

"**N**igga don't tell me, I was there...now lemme see, it was 1955..."

As we get older, we realize that history doesn't repeat itself, people do. We also find that it is during these "repeats" that sugar turns to shit and experience turns to bullshit. Hiphop is no different. Old school is back, and can't nobody find Rob Base. Damn!

People movin' out, people movin' in. Why? Because of the color of their skin? Run, run, run...but you sure can't hide.

James Brown has reached Zeus status. Thanks to the new sampling laws (that only seem to get white artists paid), he is the first Godfather to get pimped in the music industry. Shit happens, right? The history of rap, however, goes far beyond James, George and Sly. As a matter of fact—the history of rap goes beyond the music.

Back in the day, only the strong survived. Way before Fatback dropped "King Tim III" or Kool Herc and Joseph Saddler (figure that out) got busy on the one and two, the Temptations were performing "Ball Of Confusion." Back in '72, it's delivery and arrangement was closer to what we now consider rap than anything that has come after it.

An eye for an eye, a tooth for a tooth. Vote for me and I'll set you free... Rap on brotha, rap on. The only person talking 'bout love thy brotha is the preacher... Nobody's interested in learning but the teacher.

How does this come full circle? How does culture create culture? How do young M.C.'s today get on without acknowledging Duke Booty. How do D.J.s today get on without ever having "Flash To The Beat" in their crates. How do producers today get on without knowing that "Night in Tunisia" by Dizzy is the groove that started Gang Starr. Why ask why? No, real niggaz ask: Why is that? There has always been a lack of respect in America. It's just too bad that sometimes the culture creating the music falls into the same trap.

Hiphop has changed the world we live in. All of the fun and games are over, rap is now big business. It's the Amerikkkan way. No more M.C. battles, 'cause I got a Tech 9 in the saddle. No more Fresh Fest, 'cause I'm putting niggaz heads to rest. Who gives a fk about Doug E Fresh anymore, M.C. Eiaht's my nigga—he'll spray that beatboxin' Bronx bastard's guts all over the floor. Can you get with that?

The old school represents the essence. The field of dreams has now reached the hood and the old school may be our only savior. The things that Run, Bambaattaa, T La Rock, Grand Wizard Theodore, and Busy Bee did will never be done again. They were called pioneers, but the real terminology is slave. 'Cause, just like slavery has been forgotten, the "ground layers" for these new niggas gettin' paid will be forgotten too. People repeat themselves...not history. So pay attention as your life flashes before you and the GOODIE M.O.B. can't get signed for a third album ten years from now. Then you realize that the shootin' and killin' and blunt smokin' that went on in 1993 is back in style...but, only for a second. The 2003 nigga is going to create a new culture from the same culture you used to create your culture. Damn, life is a ball of confusion.

From Around The Way
Girl 2 Gansta Bitch

isa, Angela, Pamela, Renee, I love you..., you know the rest. In this day of AK47 assault rifles, Philly blunts, and the Fugees, rap music finds itself both in the forefront of and at odds with Amerikkkan society. Whoda thunk it?

Styles have changed like mood rings. Rap has gone through the transformation of being a male-dominated, female-bashing, self-proclamation of the Black male species, to the spring board of cultural awareness in a lost nation.

Back in the day when UTFO dropped "Roxanne, Roxanne," the female "evolution" in rap was born. There were many "Roxannes" out there who continued to live that life. Cool. Salt-n-Pepa, Queen Latifah, Monie Love, and Yo Yo came along and flexed skillz on the M-I-C introducing a slice of Black femalehood that had long been overlooked. It was the "nature of the sistah" that helped elevate the female MC status. Then came the transformation.

"Around The Way Girl" blew the fk up! LL gave dap to a population of females that had it goin' on for a long time, and now their image was etched on wax. The standard 9-5, uppity-fake, frontin'-on-the-flim-flam-fraud, I-got-a-degree-from-Spelman, plastic honey-dip, Madalyn Woods-wannabe, end of the road hoe was over. Thanks to Uncle L, the girlies-on-the-block got the Motts and the props needed to walk proud and let their "earrings jingle." Go 'head baby!

Enter 1993. Three years after the initial change, the hard edge of society had become evident in rap. Misogyny and California hiphop began to reshape the identity of the Black woman. Too many brothas made easy money calling women bitches on record. The white boys loved it. And while everybody was referring to the "around the way girl" as a bitch, nobody focused on the real "bitch" in this scenario: we accepted the terminology and Too Short got paid.

Now everybody's dancing. "Gansta Bitch" is a hiphop favorite, and Black women are out in their "Carhart and leather," proud to be "bitches." Rap has once again educated a pseudo-concerned culture on the correct path to step Black to the future. Concerns about ebonics will continue to grow, and thousands of lil' Bev Smiths will complain about the use of the words "nigga" and "bitch" in hiphop. This, as we have witnessed, is not scary. In the transformation of rap, the scary part is that no one is concerned about the word "Gangsta."

A Bitch is a Bitch: *Rap Sheet*, April 1995; Way Girl to Gangsta Bitch: *Agenda*, May 1993

Jesse and Jesse, Martin and Martin, and Malcolm

Jesse and Jesse

"**R**un Charlie Run. The niggers are coming! The niggas are comin'!" Forever the Black man has been running, either from something or towards something worse. As the Temptations sang in the '70's, "Charlie" (aka: the white man) only runs when he knows we up to something.

Run Jesse Run. A life's calling. For thirty years, Jesse Jackson Jr. has heard several generations of Blackness demand that his father do nothing less than that—Run. Run for something, anything! Run for Senate, run for mayor, run for president. Just keep hope alive. Jesse Jackson Jr. did just that. He heard the call and placed on himself the urgency to do something politically correct before the battle cry changed from Jesse to Colin. Sworn in by Newt, Jesse Jr. now holds the seat that Illinois Congressman Mel Reynolds vacated for his little bump and grind.

As the GOP vexes power over OPP (Our People's Problems), Jesse Jr. has quietly put himself in a position to further define his pop's career. While Illinois has become the laughing stock of Capitol Hill (Check Rep. Dan Rostenkowski, Sen. Paul Simon, and Sen. Carol

Mosley Braun), Jesse Jr. represents a new breed of politics that may save the political credibility of a state many call Ill-legal-nois.

"The next generation must take its turn," Jr. said after he was elected to serve the 2nd District of Illinois representin' Chi. "You haven't seen African Americans, at age 30, do what we've accomplished." He was right. In 75 days, the new Jackson coalition put together a campaign that saw Jesse Jr. generate more votes than five other opponents who were more experienced in politics. He shifted his weight, called on a few friends, and asked for his father's blessings. The end results were two convincing victories that put Jr. right smack in the middle of Capitol Hill.

With this victory, Jesse Jr. completes a mission that his father has been unable to accomplish: holding an important political office. But because of who his father is, and because of his "official" political inexperience, Jr. will be strapped into "playing the game" of politics once he gets to Washington. Many people will ask for many favors. That's the nature of the game, that's politics. And because he now represents the new jack Black Power Generation, he'll have to deal with the scrutiny of the Republican Party who fears that maybe the "Black planet" PE talked about is no joke.

Jesse Jackson Jr. becomes the first headstone of a post-civil rights generation that only has the Million Man March as its contribution to a movement Blackwards. He's up there alone, living for more than the city, but for the birth of a nation.

All irony set in when, the day after Jesse Jr. won the primary, his father announced that he was returning to Operation PUSH. One steps in the house, the other comes back to the fields. It's politics perfected by a family too proud and too smart to beg. A balancing of power between father and son. '90's activism. A beautiful thang. Yo "Charlie"...start runnin'.

FROM MARTIN
II MARTIN

Not the most reassuring look at Black leadership and the media.

Twenty-five years after his death, Martin Luther King reigns supreme in Africa, not Amerikkka. Recently, "real" Black peoples' two favorite magazines (*Emerge* and *The Source*) both had MLK on their April covers. Martin Luther King and Martin Lawrence (King). The former equals Legacy. The latter equals Comedy. What makes this ironic is the full circle we go through as we survive in this trap called "life." Martin Luther King represents the civil rights struggle that we have to go through to survive, and Martin Lawrence represents the cultural entertainment freedom that we struggle to attain as we try to find a reason for survival.

Over the years, the media's role in shaping Black leaders has changed. Luther (as in Martin) had to deal with limited coverage and the unsophisticated abilites of media-minds in order to gain his popularity. U No, grassroots in effect. Lawrence (as in Mar'in) has to deal with HBO, FOX, etc. and a racist, scandalous media monopoly in order to gain his following. U C,

Undaground—comedy.

The media's control over choosing Black leaders has become too dominating. Most people, especially young people, know more about Bill Belamy than they do about Hosea Williams; more about "Def Comedy Jam" than "TransAfrica"; and according to "them," more saw *Boomerang* than *Malcolm X*. At this point, it's time to panic.

The entertainment thang has been worn out. The only Blacks who receive the national exposure necessary to acquire a respectable Black-base are those Blacks, or negroes, that are in the field of dreams—oh—entertainment. The media is very wise to the fact that entertainers will always be limited in their acceptability as activists. Serious statements and activities are always overshadowed by the fact that he or she can sing, act, dance, or play ball. Seriously, what type of leader do you think Michael Jordan would be if he didn't score 30 a night?

We are not free yet—not until we find a way to seize the media-induced control over our existence and future. When was the last time you saw a non-showbiz Black person (excluding Malcolm X) on the cover of any national news medium? At the rate we're going, Eddie Murphy and Shaquille O'Neal will be "our" representatives for Prez and V.P. in 1996. The truth in this matter is that Black leaders do not emerge anymore, they are chosen—picked by a group of white men (35 at last count) who control our sources of information. Nice try Al, Louis, Dr. Jeffries, Randall, Jesse, Nelson, Maxine, Carol, and Harold (Martin, as in owner of MVP footwear—the only Black-owned gym shoe manufacturer in the country), but, 2Black + 2Strong = 4Gotten. Serious Black leaders are always placed on the back burner or are sacrificing the movement, limelighting for those who have 1/2 hour shows, 48 minute games, 60 minute records or 2-hour long performances.

In our world (Black America), civil rights has become comedy. Paul Mooney has taken the place of Dick Gregory, Bernie Mack for Malcolm X, and Martin Lawrence for Dr. Martin Luther King Jr. As followers of these "90's Niggas," it is mandatory that we pay close attention to what these "entertainers" are saying and doing. We must build upon their contributions to us. Honestly, they could be the last Black voice that you will ever hear. We know that Martin Lawrence will never be the same man that Martin King was (and it is reaching a bit to even compare the two), but if he's going to be catapulted into a leadership role then let's make sure he has the qualities to "carry the whole weight." They have "picked" the wrong brotha for the right job too many times. As far as "The 35" are concerned, all we can do is sing, dance, and maybe know Bo. Cool. Let'em think that. And until we get total control of our own "selection committee," let's make sure that we have exact leaders chosen for the love of the Black folk, and not the love of the media.

I'm neXt:
Doin' the Knowledge On The Whole "X"perience

This was a long time commin'. Never has a population of Black folks been in "Heinz ketchup" anticipation for anything quite like this. Now we in there; the movie is all that.

Now that he is gone, Malcolm is finally getting the press that he deserves (16 magazine covers in November alone); and Spike and Denzel don't have to leave the country (inside joke!). What happens now? We have been through the Malcolm Movement once before. Twice was really nice. But now that the movie is complete, and the anticipation is over—where do we go from here? The Big Question now becomes whether or not the movie can generate the same ideological-Xcitement afterwards as it did before it came to life? This will be the test to see if Black folks are for real or just doin' the "negro" thang. Where will you stand six months from now?!? May The "X" be with U.

This has been an experience, a joyride thru Blackness. Seeing Black people re-embrace Malcolm is something that should never stop under any circumstances. To you, the reader, we offer this on Malcolm:

1) Regardless of who pulled the trigger on Malcolm, his life was going to end very soon. It was simply a matter of who got to him first. Instead of focusing on who actually took Malcolm out, we need to concentrate on why he was taken. If the N.O.I. did it, so what?! If the F.B.I. did it, so what?! If the C.I.A., K.K.K., M.O.U.S.E. did it, so what?! The bottom line is that the American system killed Malcolm.

No self-determined Black man with a following and a voice who is unafraid to die will live long in Amerikkka! The only thing saving Chuck D. and Spike is that they are considered entertainers instead of activists. Malcolm X lived for the love of Black people; Malcolm X died for the liberation of Black people. The United States has a problem with men such as this— Huey, Harold, Elijah, Martin, and Fred. They make sure, for the Black man, that The Bullet or The Ballot Theory is alwayz in effect.

2) Please get the book "X": By Any Means Necessary. The Trials and Tribulations of Making Malcolm X (while ten million motherfuckers are fucking with you!) by Spike Lee and Ralph Wiley. It's deeper than the movie!

3) Don't fall into that trap of separating Malcolm and Martin. Despite their adversarial campaigns for justice, without each other they would have achieved minimal success. This is especially true for Martin. See, Martin Luther King was able to do things no other Black man or woman will probably ever be able to do again: deal with the white man and change laws at the same time.

He was able to accomplish this because Malcolm made him look "composed." And white folks did not want to deal with "uncomposed niggas." Quite as its kept, white folks really did not want to be bothered with King either. But after hearing Malcolm, they figured, "let's deal with the one without the glasses."

4) In conjunction with the editorial...FK Carl Rowan!

5) This movie will mean a lot of things to a lot of people. Judge for yourself what it means to you! Don't do that, "well Ebert and Siskel said..." or "I saw so-'n-so on Oprah, and she said..." Be real about how this movie affects you. Decide for yourself.

6) Yo, Spike, how come no Muhammad Ali in the movie?

7) Pay close attention to how the N.O.I. reacts to the movie. Brotherhood is often a hard pill to swallow. True brothers and sisters take their medicine. No movie should separate family. We need the N.O.I. to stand strong for the betterment of Black. And remember, all praises due...

8) Last but not least: At the time of his death, Malcolm X had evolved into a man of passion and concern for all people worldwide. His pilgrimage to Mecca gave him a world view, a vision that made him realize that he was not the reason the sun came up in the morning. He was no longer a "hater" of the white man. But understand this: Malcolm died only one year after he went through his last change. A year in America is not enough time to

change a man. Sooner or later, had he lived, Malcolm would have gone back to "brotha we love best," because Amerikkka has a way of making you hate white folk. By Any Means...

Jesse Jackson: *The Source*, March 1996; X Experience: *Agenda*, November 1992

YSB–
Young
Sistahs and
Brothas

SLICK AIN'T GOT NO RESPECT. . .
A Female's Perspective II

*T*he original one is gone. Tricky Dick. Richard Mil(dew)house Nixon bit the dust last month. Damn, I'm sad. I really don't know who's going to miss him, but as all slick people do, he probably left some sort of legacy (like a crooked-assed American government) behind.

I grew up watching Nixon run a shady game on America. He did nothing different than any other man would have done had he been in that position—except he got busted. Nuff said. Now I'm older, and although I don't have to "deal" with Nixon, I do have to deal with watching those brothas who think they have a game like Nixon, but won't get caught like Nixon.

Why?

Why do Black men think that they can get away with that oooh-so-sorry shit? If Watergate got exposed, if the Iran-Contra Affair got exposed, if Dan Rostenkowski got exposed, what in the hell makes brothas think that women can't expose, catch, and bust their asses?!?

Girl listen. You don't need this. Now I ain't Terry McMillan, but I will admit that a lot of Black men are sorry. Don't get me wrong, but after watching my mother, my mother's mother, my sisters, girlfriends, and women I don't even know deal with the "lame game" brothers think they can run, I feel it's time their shit got exposed.

Sistahs, if you are involved with a brotha (and I hope you are) tell him that until he begins to think like a woman, his chances of being "slick" on you are about as great as Jasmine Guy finding another job. Tell 'em to save it for the bill collectors, the student loan officers, and the cops who are chasing him. In other words, "save that drama for your mama"—y'all ain't having it.

There is no more loving individual than the Black woman. She has been through more turmoil than anyone who has ever lived on this planet. From the Virgin Mary (come on now, if Jesus was Black, what do you think she was?) to Eve to Cleopatra to Nefertiti to Harriett Tubman to Mary McCloud Bethune to Shirley Chisolm to Maya Angelou to Winnie Mandela to Maxine Waters to Queen Latifah, Black women have represented the unconditional love and strength that is often overlooked in this destructive, male dominated society.

It is men, Black men to be 'pacific (cause we say the word differently), who try to test and undermine the Black woman's strength and love and, therefore, take her kindness for granted—in order to try to get more "puddy" than they deserve.

Now, I ain't the one to get mad, upset, or pissed-off, and I ain't even the man sitting next to the woman who's sittin' next to the woman who's on some personal trip to dog brothas out. But Sistahs, I am the one who's going to run down the sloppy-brotha-syndrome to you. And if you don't know by now, you had better ask somebody:

1) If he don't come home the way he used to, he's cheating.

2) If he claims he has to work overtime and you know his ass is unemployed, he's cheating.

3) If he goes to bed with you in a different pair of underwear than he started the day in, he's cheating.

4) If he's still giving out his mother's phone number and you have been living together for a couple of years, he's cheating.

5) When your "boning" goes from three times a week to once a month, he's without a mfk'n doubt cheating!

6) If he tries that old "this number is for my boy from this girl who wanted me to hook her up with him" trick, he's cheating and he's sorry.

7) If he comes home from work and immediately takes a shower, he's clean, but he's still cheating.

8) If, all of a sudden, he gets a second beeper, he's either too cheap to buy a phone or he's cheating.

9) If, all of a sudden, he wants to wear a condom, beat his ass.

10) If he thinks he's Eddie Murphy with that "that wasn't me" shit...you know the deal.

History has consistently proven these theories to be true. Although I'm not a Black woman, I know most of these things are real. Although I have no idea what it is like to live the life of a Black woman, I do know that Black women deserve more respect than most brothas give them. Being slick means you ain't got no respect.

NIGGA PLEEZE...
a female's perspective

I'm tired. I'm tired of life, but never consider death, even though that rainbow was never enuff. I have to deal with so much shit. Society has no idea of the "land-minds" I have to walk on just to get through the day. But, like most Black women, I have no time to think about myself or my life because I have a much bigger concern: niggas and flies.

I have been told that the most difficult thing in the world is for two Black people to get along. As I've gotten older, I've realized that to be true. But I've also realized that you have to get along with somebody in order to survive. The Black man wants to believe that he can make it alone. That's bullshit. The Black woman's biggest problem is that she realize the truth and most brothas don't.

Everyone needs somebody to make it. Move as a team, never move alone, that sums it up right there. But no, you nappy-heads would rather listen to Luke, Too Short, or Snoop.

Black women and men are losing our unity. Sistahs have gone through history after history (because his story does repeat itself), waiting for the Black man to get his shit together—before he finds us. But he never does; I'm sorry—he rarely does. His excuses: "No father figure," "no male role model," "no job," "no money."

Nigga pleeze, try the truth: you got no backbone, no spine, no heart. Black men have four times as many role models as the Black woman—Jesse, Colin, Michael, Quincy, Kweisi, Louis, etc. All we got is Oprah. And why is the focus always on the young brotha who grew up without a father—young sistahs grew up in that same damn house, she needed a father too! I'm not trying to "dog" you out, but we all have problems. Stop blaming me for your problems and using me for your excuses.

Yes, you can call me a bitch, but only to my face and only when I'm acting like one. Don't use the mic or a record company to "screen" that phone call. It has become tradition to disrespect Black women, but it's always been done by someone else. We "scream" now because it hurts when it comes from you, my brotha.

Slappin' me, flippin' me and rubbin' me down ain't cool. Leaving me with our children and a "peace-out" Hallmark ain't cool. Calling me your "nubian sistah" while you're out sleeping with white women ain't cool. You know it, I know it, we know it.

I understand that Black women can be "difficult" (smile), but at least we are there—not running, not hiding and definitely not giving up on our children. Our "birth of a nation" starts with our unity, and our "death" ends with our seperation. We sistahs need companionship always, understanding most times, and support forever.

Brotha, please don't read this as an article or an essay. This is a love letter, a love letter to you. But you probably don't hear me, do you? You have another excuse, right? Nigga Pleeze...an excuse is like an asshole, everybody has one.

CHANNEL ZERO: SOAPS Vs. SPORTS

The state of the union between Black men and women can be observed through television. It is as simple as watching ABC, "All My Children" versus "Monday Night Football." Black domestic violence in full effect. News at 11.

Black men don't understand the importance of watching soap operas. Erika, Luke, Laura, and that slave-English talkin' Noah? Please!!! Too phony. But Black women—and women in general—have a grip for it. It's religion. If they miss a month (pray this doesn't happen), they have the ability to jump back into the story-line without missing a beat. To sistahs, this is intrigue; to brothas, it's insanity.

Black women don't understand the importance of watching sports. Jordan, Shaq, and Rodman's rainbow-colored hair. Come On!!! Too silly. TNT 'til 2AM. Any excuse will do. It, too, is a religion. Can't miss a month of this, it's live, but repetitive as hell. Nothing new. To brothas, this is life; to sistahs, it's death.

We only have one life to live. You know, Sony, Magnavox, VCR, and DirecTV. As the world turns and the ball bounces, we follow the tunnel-vision of others, while we refuse to take the time to understand each other.

Sports are seasonal, but Black men find a way to

"love" another sport once a season ends. From the NBA to MLB to NFL to NHL to CBA to PGA to WTA to WBA to IBF to WWF to "Real Sports" with Bryant Gumbel on HBO. And now, Tyson's back...

Soap operas aren't seasonal—they're forever, the never-ending story. From ABC to CBS to NBC to BET; from "Guiding Light" to "Days Of Our Lives" to "Sisters" to "Melrose Place" to "Savannah." Day and night. And when all else fails...talk shows. And now, Rosie O'Donnel's got a show. Thanks Oprah, for nothing.

Unfortunately, there is no bottom line or solution here, just the facts, some figures, and Nielsen ratings. Everyone is guilty, like OJ. Ooops...is that sports related or a soap opera? A happy medium. It's TV, that's how we livin'.

WHO LOVES U...BABY?

*T*hem ways, we all got 'em. Love's got nothin' to do with it. The arguments, the fights, the misunderstandings, the accusations, the rudeness, the disrespect, the finger-snappin', the backstabbin', and the "you ain't all that" attitude we deliver like the Daily News everytime we get upset with one another. For some reason, men and women love to hate each other, hate to love one another. It's so easy, so Black, so...whatever.

From Oprah to Sharazad Ali, from Cosby to OJ, the relationship between Black men and women is ill. Okay, maybe sick. It's everything but right. "Niggas ain't shit," I hear it everyday. "A bitch is a bitch," get your daily dose.

Fact or fiction—Black athletes from Mike Tyson to Warren Moon to Scottie Pippen to Lawrence Phillips to Richie Parker have a problem when it comes to dealing with women. Fact or fiction—celebrity sisters from Whoopi to Diana Ross to Imani to Diane Carroll to Lynne Whitfield have sold their souls to the flipside and have taken vows to secure that "happiness." White mentality vs. white husbands, fact vs. fiction. Let's get ready to rumble.

'Til death do we part? It's only a slogan. The excuses come like hurricanes—out of nowhere and unrelenting. Brothers claiming that sistahs drive them to be physically and mentally abusive and unfaithful. Sistahs claiming that Black men aren't capable of fulfilling their needs, wants, desires, fantasies, and credit limits at the same time. We chase the waterfalls.

Them ways. Our history has never really been a volatile one. Nor has it been one of unlove. Yes, there has been a growing misunderstanding between us, but we have always been able to rise above the nonsense to find a purpose. Before Mel Reynolds lost his goddamned mind, before Wesley brought pain to Halle, before Left Eye burned Andre Rison's crib down, before Nelson and Winnie got lost, Mom and Dad had an agenda. Purpose before understanding. Understanding before love. Love before disrespect.

When do we as Black women and men decide the worth of our relationships? When do we sit down at the table and decide that our lives together are worth something? We are trying to find love and understanding without loving and understanding ourselves. We give ourselves the wrong answers to the right questions. Sistahs scream, we're tired of "dealing" with brothas. Brothas be doin' the same. Over the years, the screams have gotten louder and louder, yet silence is the only noise we hear.

This is the hate that hate produced. Many of us now believe that loving a brotha or a sistah is more painful than showing any love at all. Black Love: It's Too Much Like Work. I can see the t-shirts and the Terry McMillan books now. Black women will fall into the shadows of rich white men, while Black men will become "successful" and find salvation, understanding, and acceptance from America's PWT. Polly wanna-craka?

Are we really that different? Why has it become so difficult for two people to get along, to be honest with each other, to be one with each other? Is this a Black thing?

Yes. Emotions and rationality separate the way we think and behave. Although stupidity often runs rampant in brotha's minds, most sistahs act on emotions. This is part of the problem. "Niggas ain't shit" because they act like they don't care. Translation: We're being rational. "A bitch is a bitch" because sistahs often get in "bitch mode" when a brotha's stupidity takes over his rationality. Translation: They scream, yell, cry, sulk, holler, eat, act cool, shop, and run up the phone bill trying to either find an answer, an excuse, or another brotha. Those are their emotional outlets. Whatever.

Then the questions pop: Why are men more secure in groups than when they're alone? Why do women offer sex when a brotha really needs some money? Why do all men think (and act) like every woman is single? Why do some women let certain brothas get away with things they wouldn't tolerate from anyone else, even their fathers? Why do sistahs automatically think brothas are unfaithful? My question... Why can't sistahs and brothas be more concerned about being happy instead of always trying to be right?

Then, there's the sex thang. We all want it. In reality, it's our biggest addiction outside of trying to be white. While we look for love in all the wrong places, we look for sex anywhere. This is where our souls get sold. There's no turning back once we mistake sex for love. An orgasm's only loyalty is to itself. Think about that. We have to realize that the enemy comes in all shapes, sizes and colors; but when it's all said and done, the enemy is never, never going to be your brotha or your sistah. Never.

Them ways. We got 'em. A harmonious conflict. Our lack of trust, understanding, honesty, and commitment to each other shouldn't be larger than the love we hold for one another. Am I expecting too much? Can't we all just get along? Yeah, I know...whatever.

PEACE, AIN'T THE WORD 2 PLAY

*T*his is a message for the fellas. G, if your girl says "peace" to you, she ain't your girl no mo! Fellas, if u are tryin' to get with a sistah and she ends the conversation with the word "peace," forget it! Your dayz iz numbered.

"Peace" has become the universal and generic exit-line. Women have picked up on this and have utilized it to their advantage. Yeah, it's a gender thang now! See, brothas use the word all of the time (sometimes for no reason at all). Sistahs, on the other hand, use the term in reference to friendship. The only time a female will use "peace" in ending a conversation is if she considers u a platonic friend. Boyfriends, husbands, bonin' partners, sugar-daddys, etc. get the sensitive-your-my-man-exit-line of "later baby," or "bye sweetheart." But ain't no Black woman in her right mind gonna tell a man she's interested in "peace." She saves that for the homies and the homettes.

By nature, Black women are not naughty. They pay attention to everything they do and say. If a woman says "peace" to u...y'all will be friends for a long time. And u might as well forget about the booty, it ain't yours. Some other brotha's got it. She tells him, "bye." He's in tha houze. Can u dig what I'm sayin'?

Know the code. By now I know the sistahs are rollin' in the aisles, trippin' because part of their game just got peeped. Brothas are probably scratchin' their heads wonderin', "what the hell is this fool talkin' about?" Sistahs know, been knowin'. They also know that one day we'll catch on. So...until then, we have to understand: Brothas, watch out for the word "peace" when it comes from the mouth of a female. It's the biggest one-word hint she can give u. There's nothing intimate about the word. It's almost as dangerous as, "my friend." And I know u know what I'm talking 'bout. But if u don't, check it. Ask the *u know* sistahs if they tell their men P-E-A-C-E before they hang up the phone or before they go to sleep.

If you find any....THEY'RE LYIN'!

Louis and Khallid, Harold and David, and Allen

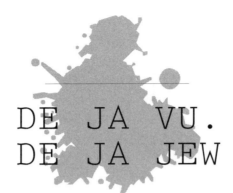

DE JA VU.
DE JA JEW

"Who is it sucking our blood
in the Black community?
A white impostor Arab and a
white impostor Jew."
—Brother Khallid Muhammad

On November 29, Brother Khallid Muhammad snapped. He unleashed one of those rare, treasured speeches that either scares the hell out of you or makes you laugh. If you are a follower of the man, you'll know that this wasn't even one of his best speeches. He's always been a masterful speaker, and an accurate one. But on this day in New Jersey, he WENT OFF!!! It seemed as if someone had made Khallid mad, and he used this speech to say things so mean-spirited that it was funny.

But unfortunately, some people didn't laugh. The Anti-Defamation League (white Amerikkka's underground watchdog group) screamed foul. When that didn't work, they screamed intentional foul. That didn't work either, so the ADL decided to jump stereotypical and excercised their power the best way they knew: Money.

On January 20, the ADL ran a full page ad in the most expensive media outlet in the country, *The New York Times*. The ad simply reprinted excerpts from Khallid's speech that was now two months-old. Now they got what they were "reaching" for; they got that response. Technical Foul! Another Black civil war open for public discussion. Welcome to Hymietown.

The Black life cycle goes and comes in thirty year intervals. 1900, 1930, 1960, 1990. Every thirty years or so, Black America goes through some dramatic self-awareness change aka: a gut check. From the building of Black businesses and hospitals to the great depression to the civil rights movement to Afrocentricism. Thirty years ago, the Honorable Elijah Muhammad had a "problem" with Brother Malcolm X. Malcolm's voice was large in New York and his reputation was spreading across the country. Today, the Honorable Louis Farrakhan has a "problem" with Brother Khallid Muhammad. Khallid's voice is large in Los Angeles and his reputation is spreading across the country. Malcolm spoke at Harvard. Khallid spoke at Kean. Malcolm appeared on 60 Minutes. Khallid appears on Ice Cube's album. 1964. 1994. Elijah Muhammad was forced to make a decision regarding one of his ministers because of "remarks made." Louis Farrakhan was forced to do the same. Silence Malcolm. Denounce Khallid. 1964. 1994. De ja vu. De ja jew.

THE SPEECH: "We don't owe the white man nothing in South Africa. He's killed millions of our women, our children, our babies, our elders...If he don't get out of town by sundown, we kill everything white that ain't right...after they're dead, we go to the graveyard and dig them up and kill them again because they didn't die hard enough."

THE TRUTH: Nothing like this is ever going to happen. In the two months since Brother Khallid delivered these words, not one of the 150 students present has gone to South Africa and murdered white folks. Straight up, if Black people in South Africa—and anywhere else for that matter—haven't started killing white people after all these years, it ain't gonna happen after hearing or reading this speech. The problem is that white people are scared that the wrong "niggas" will hear something like this and go Colin Ferguson-crazy. Little do they know that Black society is so dysfunctional and divided that we couldn't spark a collective riot beyond South Central if we wanted to. But that's another story.

THE PROBLEM: Large white organizations, especially the ADL, love to "instigate" fights. And this was a good one to start. Watching "niggers" argue and put each other down in public gives them orgasms. Just like the Signfyin' Monkey, they pick a fight, ignite a fight, watch and enjoy the fight without being in the fight. It's classic, it's masterminded, and it's getting old.

The situation is indicative of so many other "rumbles" that tear at the foundation of the Black world community. WE SIMPLY NEED TO HANDLE OUR OWN PROBLEMS ON OUR OWN TIME! Yes, Brother Khallid may have said some wicked things about every non-

Black walking the face of the earth, but why does an "outside" organization have to determine how and when we handle this problem? It's a Black thang, stay the fk out!!! If the Black community really felt that this problem was worth addressing then we would have done so on November 30th.

THE SOLUTION: The Black Press, if there truly is one, needs to be overtly demanding in setting the agenda for Black America. The *Afro-American* or the *City Sun* needs to decide when we deal with our "internal" problems, not *The New York Times*. *Emerge*, not *Time*. BET, not ABC. Black leaders (hold up, let's count 'em: 1,2... STOP! That's it.) need to tell some of these white "power brokers" to kiss their ass when they demand comments on Black issues. In particular, Farrakhan needs to handle this situation the same way the president of AT&T handled using a monkey and Africa together as a marketing tool in their employee's magazine: handle it behind closed doors with a sign that says, "No whites allowed."

THE AFTERMATH: What comes out of situations like this is dissension. The "divide and conquer" rule is in full effect. Black folks now have to choose between the greater of two goods. Khallid or Louis? Malcolm or Elijah? Ali or Tyson? Let's just hope the situation doesn't totally unfold like it did in '64.

THE CONCLUSION: This is simply a situation of BIG bank take little bank. The ADL and other white "power brokers" in this country are probably the only groups who have the economic power to buy ad space like Ross Perot buys air time. They have the money to "instigate" any fight they want, without ever wondering where their next dollar is coming from. Black people do not have that luxury.

The ADL needs to be recognized for what it truly is: a paranoid, self-centered, anti-Black spy organization. Ask Abraham Foxman, national director of the ADL, why the press (which the "bloodsuckers" control) didn't focus on the anti-Arab or anti-Asian remarks in Khallid's speech?

But as usual the situation was blown way out of proportion. On the Blackside, we need to worry about our future. How many times are we going to allow "outsiders" the liberty of coming in "our house" and calling the shots? When is the N.O.I. going to honestly tell the ADL to bacdafucup? When is the Black press going to run an ad on what South Carolina Senator, Fritz Holland, said about "niggers?" Who is going to be strong enough to continue to follow Brother Khallid Abdul Muhammad? Is Captain Yusuf going to put a "hit" out on Khalid? Is 1994 going to be 1964?

DO U EVER THINK ABOUT WHEN U OUTTA HERE?

New York City, listen up: YOU FK'D UP! Not getting David Dinkins back in office will haunt you for a very, very...very long time. Trust me, a brotha from Chicago, I know.

A Black mayor has always been sort of a status quo. The position really doesn't hold much power, but it gives Black people hope. How then, after watching what happened to us in Chicago, could New York (or any other city for that matter, except Boston or Phoenix) let this opportunity slip away?

Being the "first" Black mayor is a job nobody wants except for the people who ain't running. Chicago's first Black mayor, Harold Washington, held the position with dignity. For the first time in Chi-Town's history, Black people felt that we had accomplished something large. Forget what happened once he got in there, our job was to KEEP him in there. We failed. Harold was killed...oh, I'm sorry, I mean he died.

Confusion set in, and Black Chicago didn't know what to do, where to go, who to trust, or better yet—

who to vote for. Outta control and kicking each other in the ass, we let a Klansman (or the son of one, you choose) back in. And this is where the story begins...

Ed Koch ran New York the same way that Richard (Big Dick) Daley ran Chicago, with an iron fist and a rope with a noose at the end. City Official or City Overseer? For over 20 years, Daley ingeniously ran an apartheid system and renamed it "The Machine." Koch—like Richard (Little Dick) Daley—was too stupid to camouflage his disdain for niggers. After 12 years of dealing with Koch, how could New York leave the door open for this to happen again?

The issue here is solidarity. When it comes to election time, color means everything! White folks, if they fear a loss of power, will vote for Ren or Stempy, or even Bernie Epton, just to keep Black folks out. They don't care what is said, what morals this person stands on, or how much money he or she has stolen. Their collective objective is to "keep the niggers out of office." And trust me New York; once it's done, it's DONE.

Bed-Stuy do or die is dead. Even though David Dinkins may not have been the best man for the job, he was better than Koch, Lindsey, and most definately, Guliani.

True representation will be harder to find now. Your city will win a basketball championship and become politically complacent. Small Black businesses will move out of Fort Greene to Manhattan, and Spike Lee will get an Oscar and quit filmmaking because he'll "have nothing left to prove" (aka: Jordan). Yeah, the city will look better, but see how many Black people will get those three-year, $40 billion contracts to add another lane to the Brooklyn Bridge, or better yet, the "Jersey

Turnpike." It will be amazing. You'll see all those white folks working, tearing up city streets and highways and putting them back together again, weekly. Ah yes, as one white man said, "the good ol' days."

We're sorry New York. Sorry you didn't learn from our mistake. For once, we set an example, and you chose to follow it. Damn. Go visit City Hall now, and look at how much more confident white people have become. They realize that you messed up too. They understand that sometimes it's better for them to be pro-white than to be pro-human.

This is not something to think about; this is something to feel. The effects of this will last much longer than Arsenio Hall's television show. From this point on, all you can do is watch others "seem" happy while you kick yourself. Trust me, take it from a city that knows. The color of your skin can only hurt you if you let it. The color of white skin has been hurting you (well, all of us) since day one. You just played their game. It's called Outta Here; aka: POLITICS. Impossible to win, but very, very easy to lose.

Good luck in 2001.

AMERICA'S MOST WANTED (IVERSON AND THOMPSON)

When John Thompson speaks, people don't listen—they shake in their boots. I know I did. To get on his bad side is a feeling beyond fear. For a brief ten minutes I was there, but I lived to tell about it. Coach Thompson, in the most elegant of stern speeches, presented the rules for talking to his "son." I listened. He continued. I shook. I felt like his own kid. At the time, I wished I was—maybe the fear would have been reduced. Only Coach knows the power he holds.

Protective custody is what most sons want from the people who are in the position to nuture, direct, and raise them. Not to raise the issue of African American males running scared, but Allen Iverson is lucky. He has what most of us don't—a pops; a father figure. He has a man in his life to help him deal with the reality of being...a man. Iverson, the most gifted, talented, and in-demand basketball player in America, has found that "one-man protection plan" in the form of John

Thompson—an institution of learning and direction. Most brothas can't even go there. We can't comprehend. Unless you've grown up fatherless, you don't truly understand. We ghetto bastards ask the same question every day of our lives: Who can I run to when I need love?

Escape to nowhere...anywhere, but never run. Allen Iverson needs an answer; Georgetown University has one. Depending on the direction, Washington, DC is either heaven or hell—Dark Country or Chocolate City. Georgetown, however, is neither. For now, it is simply the answer. Understand that Iverson did not run here. He simply took advantage of the best opportunity life ever offered him. He left high school as the best ball player (including football, where he was AP Player of the Year in Virginia) in the country—easily. He had abilities that Charlie Ward could only dream about. Iverson was, and still is, a legend-icon in Hampton, Virginia.

How good was Ive? Kansas University's coach, Roy Williams, who was once Michael Jordan's assistant coach at North Carolina, said that Iverson "might be the best guard I've ever seen."

Georgetown University is strongly represented in the hood. City to city, block to block, chain nets to no nets, young Black urbanites frontin'. Gray and blue triple goose down jackets and Starter caps. Nike replicas and Champion sweats: Georgetown. One of America's most prestigious, private, catholic institutions has found a place in the hood. Ever since they introduced the world to Patrick Ewing and Michael Graham, Georgetown has been the Black school of choice for every shorty who 1) can't afford to go there, 2) doesn't have the grades to get in, 3) has no intention of going to college in the first place, and 4) needs John Thompson as their father figure. Everybody wants to be down, but nobody can. Allen Iverson grew up as one of these brothas—he just got lucky.

Stuart Gardens, baby! Low income housing in Virginia. Nothin' but love. Allen Iverson was raised there with his two sisters. At the tender age of 15, his mom, Ann, began to take care of what was rightfully hers. Her son's life has been a roller coaster. He has had to deal with everything from his best friend's murder to visits from former NAACP national chairman, Ben Chavis. The true gamut. Heaven and hell. He has always been his family's best chance for escape. Along with his talent and his youth, Allen has had the unreal responsibility of doing what keeps many of us back—being raised and raising a family at the same time. In most cases, this would be a Black thing, but since Allen has beaten the odds and has made it to G'Town (instead of walkin' around the neighborhood, frontin', and wantin' to be a superstar in a Hoya t-shirt), it's an Allen thing...you wouldn't understand.

November 1995. Nothing is ever the same. Walk into the lobby of McDonough gymnasium on Georgetown's campus and you'll notice the difference. Oh yeah, the enormous, ever-so-deep framed photo of Fred Brown and Gene Smith with the 1983 NCAA National Championship trophy is still the centerpiece, and Ewing's, Mourning's, and Mutombo's reign still towers over all of the rest. But, on the floor—in the glass enclosed trophy case—the change is evident. Two solid gold basketballs chill. Trophies. One reads: "Allen Iverson 1994-95 Big East Rookie-of-the-Year"; the other, "Allen Iverson 1994-95 Big East Defensive Player-of-the-Year." A letter from President Clinton sits between the two trophies.

Inside the gym, Daddy is home. His voice echoes. It's year two in the beginning of John Thompson's new life. Papa's got a brand new bag; a bag of tricks in baggy shorts. See, Allen Iverson is not the same player that walked into this gym twelve months ago. He's controlled, confident, and well-coached. Like father, like son; like son, like father. Last year, John Thompson learned as much about Allen Iverson as Ive learned about Coach. By being the first truly celebrated player under 6'12" in the history of the Thompson era, Iverson was the solution to his "father's" problems.

"Coach (Thompson) is like a father figure to me. Right off hand...we just clicked." Allen Iverson's words are soft, but they run deep. He understands that not only is he getting one of life's greatest educations, but he's also filling a void in the career of a man who knows more about turning boys into men than Michael Bivins.

"Ninety percent of having a relationship with him is things that occur off the court," said Iverson. "He helped me through last year. I didn't want to come here and just do anything. Any problems that I have, I can go to him and he'll sit down and listen. It is a lot more than player-coach between us. I don't think I could've made it (through last year) without him."

Thompson takes the yellow-brick road with Allen. He knows he has someone special; a gift, but that it's not just about basketball.

"If you've been in this business for awhile," Thompson says when asked about his prodigal son, "you know you're not supposed to be impressed with people. You're here to attempt to mold and get (students) prepared for their next stage of life. That's what education is all about. Allen has done just that. He has done what I've asked him to do, and when he has not done it, we've sat down and talked.

"He understands that he wants to educate himself. So it's not a problem. It's almost amusing to me sometimes to hear the questions I'm asked about him in relation to the person that I have to deal with."

It's always that way. Nobody understands true talent, especially those talented players who are deemed Thompson's sons.

If last year was Iverson's coming out party, then this year should be his throwdown, all-night-long, block party affair. Last year's Big East new jack is now expected to be the player president. He's a college sophomore going on year five in the NBA. Believe the hype. Iverson is expected to equal Toby Bailey's phenomenal game in last year's final for UCLA. All of a sudden, after one season of blowin' up the spot, Allen Iverson is expected to be the greatest son a father could ever have. He just may be.

Summer ball'n in New York—where legends are built. This summer Iverson went mythical; beyond legendary. Able to get loose in an NBA atmosphere, Iverson was able to put his whole package together and show all the critics what basketball is about. He averaged close to 50 points a game against teams that included a host of NBA players. On three occasions, he scored over 70 points. He told the coach, during the third quarter of a game, down by 26, with only 20 points, to give him the ball every time down court. Result? Victory. And, oh yeah, Allen finished with 81 points. Believe it.

"Yeah, I did," responds Iverson to the legendary tales of summer madness. "I think I play a lot better in a NBA style. It is wide open, run 'n gun, man-to-man all game—and that's the game I like to play."

On the other hand, he changed gears and ran everything during the World University Games in Japan. In a more controlled environment, playing with Ray Allen, Tim Duncan, Charles O'Bannon, Dametri Hill, Kerry Kittles and so on, Iverson led the team in scoring (16.7), assists (6.1), and steals (3.0). He shot 56 percent from the floor, scored 26 points in both the semifinal and gold medal games, and led the USA to another international victory.

Try to defend Iverson, he'll make you feel lost—like high school geometry. He'll eat you up like meat, and have you praying he turns vegetarian. He has quickness that makes Michael Johnson seem slow.

At times, however, his speed can be his worst enemy instead of his greatest asset. He'll provide more flashes of greatness in one game than Ken Griffey Jr. did against the Yankees in the playoffs. But, uncontrolled speed was once Iverson's nemesis. Until now, maybe.

"A lot of times, I get caught up in the hype of the game and get out of control sometimes," Ive says. "Now, I'm working hard on being patient, a lot more than I was last year. I made a lot of freshman-type mistakes, but I matured as the season went on and I learned a lot of things from game to game."

"That's the thing Coach talks to me about now, the leadership role and being able to run this team. The point guard position is supposed to be the focal point and run the show, and that's what I have to do (for this team) if I'm ever to think about playing at the next level."

Everybody's mind is on the next level, except Allen's. See, most people don't know Allen. They don't get the chance. This is a good thing. The world is no more ready for Allen than he is ready for the world. He is a genius, trying to stay focused and appreciative at the same time. He's being told to keep his visions limited but not to underestimate himself. It's the Georgetown paradox. He's a genuinely soft-spoken kid whose "first love" is football ("I miss the game so much"). He's a B-average Fine Arts student who, in his spare time, does caricatures of famous people he has met, including other basketball players and his teammates. He sees Kenny Anderson, Timmy Hardaway, and Nick Van Exel in his game. He says that his crossover is his lethal weapon. "It's effective. Even if I don't catch the opponent with it all the way, it's enough to get me by them."

He's a young Black man searching for a way out of the shadows of darkness which almost ended his movement before it even started. A few years ago, the racially motivated brawl which resulted in his felony conviction was over-publicized, well-documented, un-called for, and ill-fated. It doesn't define him the way it defines society. Honestly, Allen needed Johnnie Cochran for protection. Case closed.

He accepts the burden as "just another responsi-bility" a young brotha must deal with in order to survive.

"I can accept all of the tags people give me," he says after a season of dealing with ignorant fans yelling "go back to jail," calling him "OJ," and schools playing "Jailhouse Rock" during time-outs at basketball games.

One time, it got so ugly that Coach Thompson, being pops on the spot, had to take matters into his own hands by refusing to play a game until the opposition began "acting civilized."

Through this, Allen's age of innocence finds its depth. He's in so much control off the court that it's scary. When other brothas would be annoyed, angered, and well...pissed, Allen remains calm, just like his "father" taught him. Life, not basketball, will carry you through.

"What makes a good person," he says, "is being able to bounce back from all the difficulties and keep going." Wisdom from a 20-year-old who is no longer in no-man's land because he is a man.

That which does not kill us only makes us stronger. In other words, "You go boy!" Allen carries a different type of pride in his heart and mind. Now, he no longer has to carry it solo. On the court, he'll have Othella Harrington and Jerome Williams to help him become the Big East Player-of-the-Year and the NCAA Defensive Player-of-the-Year. Off the court, Coach Thompson will help Allen fight off the rumors—and persuasion—of turning pro after the season. Wherever he goes he'll probably be the number one pick. His future could be so much more damaging and out of control than his past, which is frightening. Through the exploitation of his situation, Allen is about to run into a game called life. He's fortunate to have "big poppa" as his guide, his protection, his father for life—or at least for the next two years.

The Answer. He slips the grey Kente-trimmed

number 3 uniform over his head. The five letters—HOYAS—spread across his chest like a shield; a badge of honor. Although he is right handed, his left arm carries the answer—a tattoo in the form of a bulldog. Above the mascot ("a coincidence," he says) are two simple words:

THE ANSWER. The symbolism. The logic. As his frail, 6'0" 175 pound body prepares to go to war, you begin to truly realize that nothing is missing. Nothing. Every aspect of his game, from offense to defense, is complete.

Coach Thompson, towel in check, calls Allen to the sideline. A simple pat on the back of the head speaks volumes. That's the power he has. Allen breathes deep. He maintains control and continues to do his thing like no one else. John Thompson lives for this. This is his "son." He's proud. Thompson and Iverson. Cliff and Theo. Some guys have all the luck, and some, well, they just deserve it.

De Ja Jew: *Agenda*, June 1994; America's Most Wanted; *Slam*, November 1995

ESPN: Negro

SLAVERY 1994:
A DREAM DEFERRED

"I don't believe in role models, but you're mine."
—*Charles Barkley to Chris Webber after the slam.*
Basketball has always been more than a game to African Americans. Many times it has been a means to an end. Young brothas have always used ball skills as an "excuse" to take them and their families into the promised land. It's almost a religion.

For every one brotha that makes it, there are hundreds that don't. For every one Larry Johnson, there are four Alfredrick Hughes', eight Billy Harris', and twenty-five Fly Williams'. The odds are against you from the beginning. But since basketball is the most cost-effective sport available to urban America, brothas gravitate to it and excel at it.

In Deerfield, Illinois, Nike held a conference for the country's top high school basketball players. The Nike Scholastic Festival attempted to take the extra steps necessary to build a better foundation—math, english, and life skill classes—for the deferred dreams of high school athletes.

Cool, but the young men came wanting to make it

to "the league." Reality check: of the 140 high school basketball players invited to "show and prove" who was the man, only 12 are probably ever going to receive a check with (NBA Commissioner) David Stern's signature at the bottom. This is the truth that the kids did not want to hear.

They came to play ball and have fun, with no NCAA coaches, no pro scouts, no World Cup, no OJ, and, thank God, no Dick Vitale around. This is what "kids" are supposed to do. Learning and hearing the "hard" facts of life is not what summer vacations and basketball camps are all about. Yo Nike, could you JUST DO...something else.

On July 4th at 2:15PM, Gee Gervin, son of the "Iceman," George Gervin, is putting on a shootin' spree. One, bam! Two, bam! Three, bam! Like that damn bunny, he keeps going. Four. Five. Rimmmmming...yes, six. Bam! 35 feet out! It's unbelievable. Then he misses. Chasing down the loose ball at half court, he looks up, sees his teammate DeJuan Vasquez in front of him, smiles, then pulls up—bam—seven through the net.

Performances like this are how legends are made. Too bad Gee's performance took place during the warm-ups, because a big part of legend status is execution when the time comes. If you don't believe me, ask John Starks.

The scenario here is scary. From inside the walls of deception, I watched all of my mistakes come back to life. I watched over a hundred Black men fall for the "I Love This Game" paradox. Hoping and dreaming that one day their skills can pay the bills. The same dream I had in 1980 (which ended in '85 on a semi-pro team in

Louisiana) is going ever-so strong in 1994. Only this time, corporate America is at the helm, and skills are only part of the game.

Growing up and ballin' on the playgrounds of Chicago teaches a brotha that either you're going to make it or you ain't. There's no in between. I was lucky, because at 5'6", I realized the deal before I was able to vote. I can't say the same for our future. Not here, not now.

"Almost everybody here is here for a reason and most of it has nothing to do with basketball," says Todd Harris, one of the camp's referees/counselors. "These kids are depending on this game to make them live. Most of their families are depending on it too. A lot of them have no idea what's next after the ball stops bouncing. In their hometowns, people tell them everything they want to hear: 'Oh, you're so great' and 'You're the best that's ever played here.' You know. The people around these kids don't love them. They have no life instruction. In a way I feel sorry for some of them."

"But what about K.G.?"

"Oh, he has other problems. He's hard-headed (smile), but he's almost the exception to the rule."

K.G. is a fool. Kevin Garnett, at times, acts more like the jokester from the local biddy squad than the number one high school basketball player in the country. If he grew up around my way, "Loud & Proud" is what we would have called him.

"Rewind that, rewind that!" Garnett screams as we all watch the Nike video. "Check this out. Around-the-back...Ugh! Slam on Barkley. That's what I'm talkin' about!"

Watching Chris Webber do his now infamous dunk

on Sir Charles excites Garnett. There is something about the ex-University of Michigan superstar that Garnett sees in himself. Maybe it's the fact that they possess the same infectious smile, along with the size, strength, and agility to make fans ogle and opponents envious? Maybe it's the fact that they are the epitome of the new youth movement, representing the future of the hardwood? Let Nike tell it...maybe it's the shoes?

But in basketball, sometimes being ranked number one don't mean shit. Sometimes—most times—it's about who has the best game. Being able to "play ball" and "having game" are two totally different things. K.G. found this out the hard way. For the first time in two years at Nike's basketball camp, his squad lost. They lost to a team of youngsters who proved that press clippings, large followings, and scholarship offers mean nothing when you've got something to prove.

Stacked with "two-handfuls of unheard ofs" the team from California took out Garnett's number one ranked team—which included Ron Mercer, the number two ranked player in the country—and proceeded to turn the small town of Deerfield out.

Now, there have been a fair share of championship teams in this gym (play took place at the Berto Training Center, practice facilities for the Chicago Bulls), but none quite this young, or this surprising. Led by a 6'5" senior point guard (Olujimi Mann) and a 6'5", 210 pounds, 16 year-old sophomore (Schea Cotton), they put fear into the hearts of those that faced them. Unugly like the Knicks, the California "dream team" made a lot of people believe that the future of the game may not be as dismal as it looked on NBC last spring or on 125th Street in Harlem last night. They almost made the dream worth living.

"I'm glad I know that I belong," says LaRon Profit. You know, you come here hoping that all of the hype is real and then you just want to see if you can compete." LaRon Profit has a basketball name. Some names just sound good. LaRon Profit is one of those names. Looking like a kinda-slender version of the old-school Magic Johnson (another phat b-ball name), Profit dropped knowledge. "Even though I had some off games, I know that I am one of the better ball players in the country. That's cool with me. That's all I wanted to find out. For myself, you know. Trust me, I'm not like everybody else here. I want to find a job when I get home. Straight basketball camps ain't gonna make it."

Rob Williams, on the other hand, is different. He is basketball. "Yo Scoop, you wanna be my agent?" Williams is a point guard extraordinaire. At 5'10" with a two-inch Afro, he has Kenny Anderson skills with Reggie Miller confidence. He's the perfect example of what happens to an unknown kid who comes to one of these camps and blows-up.

"Man, some of these cats are scrubs! How did they get in here? Before the camp, they said I had everything but a jumper. So I worked on my shot. 100, maybe 200 shots a day. Now I'm the man (laugh). I'm the best point guard in the country. Now I didn't see everybody play, but I'm going to be ranked by the time this camp is over." Nuff said, and after watching him play—he may be right.

But the delusion is still there. I'm not saying that he won't make it, but even he questioned, how many Division 1 schools are going to invest in a 5'10" point guard?

Talent has always been the mainstay in the ghetto-centric version of American economics. America business has found hundreds of ways to profit on the talent of it's Black youth. Most recently, rap and basketball have been its greatest profit producers. Only through sports, especially basketball, are you encouraged to "abort" your education for a high paying position with a Fortune 500 company. Do you think IBM and the NBA have the same requirements and training programs for their incoming employees? Doubt it.

Education aside, basketball has built more careers for those who don't understand what a career is and how long it is supposed to last. Everybody wants to be like Mike, but nobody wants to be like Mike's boss. Nobody wants to hear the truth that Mike ain't really the man, but the talent-less, four-degree havin' Rhodes Scholar is the man who runs shit. That pill is a little too big to swallow.

Nike's participation in this conference shows that they are concerned, but, will they hire any of these kids if they don't make it in the NBA? All week long you could hear the screams.

"Man, we're tired of this. We don't get a break," screamed a group of players during breakfast. "Up at 6 a.m. to eat, then to class! We don't get to play ball until two. If I wanted to go to summer school I would have stayed at home. This is supposed to be my vacation, or something. I ain't coming back next year."

The reality is that neither will a lot of the others. Only 20% of the kids at this camp will finish college, less than that will make it to "the league."

Richie Parker is pissed.

"Ron, I gave you the lane for a dunk, and you didn't dunk it!"

Parker is the pride of New York right now. He has an effortless game that can make opposing teams self-destruct. Ron Mercer has a similar game. And even though he looks better than the rest of the ball players here [Note: I hate pretty brothas that are nice on the hoop, they make you look bad on the court then walk off with your woman], he still gets respect for never disrespecting anybody—even his boy Parker, who wanted to see him dunk on him while they were guarding each other in a game.

Too bad the same can't be said for Derek Hood. His mission was strictly disrespect. An hour ago he showed his ass (not literally) by outplaying Ron Mercer and the rest of the squad, in a straight-up pride-on-the-line big-showdown game. See, there's a difference in a heart-breaker and a heart-taker.

The list can continue. DeJuan Vazquez, Glendon Henderson, Ronnie Fields, Sam Okey, Bobby Joe Evans, Vincent Carter, Larry Allaway, Charles Hathaway, Derek Hines, Cory Benjamin, etc.; all have the ability to be the next Shawn Kemp, Anfernee Hardaway or Alonzo Mourning. Who, though, is in position to be the next Ted Turner, Jerry Riensdorff, or Julius Erving? The question remains as to whether or not they have the insight, knowledge, and heart to be Heir off the court or simply air on the court? It's going to take a lot of work, because the struggle to keep basketball "attractive" to the business community starts when companies sponsor camps that are run as meat markets which showcase kids who have no idea what the hell is going on.

This year, the attendees at Nike's "conference" spent as much (if not more) time in english and math classes, and listening to the "life lessons" of NBA Vice

President of Operations Gary Brokaw, BJ Armstrong, Bobby Dandridge, and Nike "godfather" Forrest Harris, than they did on the basketball court. This year it was time to P.L.A.Y. (Particpating in the Lives of America's Youth.) Nike did that, and so did Schea Cotton. But in a world where dreams need to be re-directed more than they need to be encouraged, a t-shirt, a couple of classes, and a basketball are not gonna make it.

So how do you defer a dream? I don't know, but developing a jump shot is a damn good start.

Mission
Impossible

Outside of the Chicago Bulls locker room, Allen Iverson is locked in conversation. He is surrounded by white men in suits.

He stands quietly and listens to the words rolling from the mouths of the people so "concerned" about his future. As I approach Allen, he reaches out and gives me a hug. I jokingly whisper in his ear, "I see you keepin' good company." He laughs and he's out. On to meet Jordan.

Attorney Kevin Poston is pissed. His company, PSP, just lost another Black superstar to a white agent. Iverson has signed with David Falk. Poston never even had a chance to talk to Iverson. "It's one thing to say who's the best agent," laments Poston, "but it's another thing to say who's the best agent for that kid."

Poston isn't the only one heated. Black sports agents across the country are disturbed about the growing trend of top Black talents rolling to white agents. Say's one Black agent, "white agents are snatching up prize clients faster than we used to snatch up cotton." Of the top ten players selected in the NBA draft lottery this year, none were represented by Blackness. On Dream Team III, only three of the twelve NBA players (Penny Hardaway, Mitch Richmond, and Gary Payton) had Black agents. In total, close to 70% of the players in the NBA are represented by white agents, but, this ain't about Black men bitchin'.

It's a helluva thing to be the best and still be overlooked because of your race by your own people. It's Black-on-Black crime at the corporate level. For instance, three Black agents, Dr. Charles Tucker, Eugene Parker, and Kevin Poston are among the best in business. Parker's Deion Sanders deal shook up the world in a way Ali never could, and Tucker still has people tripping over his "alleged" $100M coup for Glenn "Big Dog" Robinson. Poston's Penny Hardaway deal, which at the time was one of the largest sports contracts ever, is still considered an industry "classic." That's hard work; that's brilliance.

In addition to having a solid track record, Black agents are often more qualified than their white counterparts. Many Black agents are attorneys. Many white agents, however, are just men with few qualifications trying to make a bundle of money off Black talent. And while most are content to earn their 10% percent, some have used their positions of trust to do things that are not in the best interest of their meal tickets.

White athletes hire white agents; Black athletes hire white agents. What's wrong with this picture? Since most agents advise their clients on where to live, how to live, where to invest their income, and even what charities to support, how Black is Black when whitey is pulling the strings? The lack of Black representation is not only damaging to the viability of Black agents, but also the ability of African Americans to exercise power at the highest level of professional sports—when David Falk talks, David Stern listens.

The real question is, how detrimental is this to the best interest of the Black athletes themselves?

"Over 20 of the brothas coming into the NBA next year have no college degrees," said Dana London, executive director of Transition Team, a not-for-profit life-skills organization designed to bridge the gap of socialization and economics of the Black athlete prior to turning pro. "The NCAA, the agents, the teams...none of them is remotely interested in these kids getting smarter, or being able to care for themselves once their playing days are over. It somewhere becomes our job to look out for one another, because ultimately we are the only ones who really know how much we stand to lose. We've been there. Many of the white agents haven't."

Kevin Poston agrees: "History has taught us that sometimes we need to take care of ourselves. Whites may set up programs, but they may not always be the best programs for us. David Falk isn't hiring any brothas to work with him, just those to work for him. If we turn the tables and the athlete is white and the agent is Black, the white athlete wouldn't give that competent Black agent the time of day."

Despite the criticisms leveled at Black players with white agents, the root cause of the problem doesn't lie at the player's Nikes. How much responsibility can be put on a 19-year old in choosing who truly has his best interest at heart?

"A lot of it starts with the coaches," says Len Elmore, president and CEO of Precept Sports and Entertainment, Inc." Sometimes financial arrangements are made before they get to us. That makes it very difficult for us (Black agents) to play. It's not about being racist, it's simply about being able to play with a fair hand."

"He's right, but it goes further than that," says Kevin Poston. "It becomes a matter of responsibility. We know we're not going to get the same chances as the white firms because they have white universities and coaches supporting them and not recommending us— no matter what we do." And which sports agents does Rick Pitino or Dean Smith recommend his players talk to? Which sports agents does John Thompson support?

Sadly enough, Black coaches play a major role in the perpetuation of the status quo. "I love John Thompson," Poston continues, sounding more idealistic than nationalistic. "But, what happened with Allen Iverson hurt me. That's why I was upset. No Black agency or agent even got the chance to interview Iverson. It has nothing to do with him going to Falk, it has more to do with none of us getting a chance to even talk to a potential first-rounder who has a Black coach that already knows what we (Black agents) are up against.

It comes down to a matter of accountability. The Black Coaches Association is one of the most influential bodies in the NCAA. Most of its members take on the responsibility of not only coaching Black players, but also becoming father figures and guidance counselors. Given their powerful influence on their young players decision making process, it is imperative that these coaches be aware and "assist" the Black agent in getting a fair shot at signing some of their players. The Black coaches must understand that if they and the Black athlete does not believe in, support, and employ the Black agent, nobody else will. It's not like John Stockton is about to do it.

The "every brotha is his brotha's keeper" policy becomes very difficult to follow when dollar signs are attached. The resistance to Black representation in sports, particularly in basketball, has more to do with laws of "anti-trust" than lack of consciousness or responsibility. Black people must learn to have faith in their own. The parents of young Black athletes must learn that there are professional Black business people out there who take their sons' best interest to heart. Black coaches must be willing to become a liaison between Black agents and their players, making them aware of the great job the agents have done for the athletes who came before them. And what about the future stars of the NBA? They must overcome a 400 year-old myth: "the white man's water may not be any wetter, but it sure does tastes better."

SCHOTT IN THE DARK

What's the difference between a white police officer in Los Angeles and a baseball team owner in Cincinnati? Not much, both get off the hook for treating Blacks any way they feel Blacks should be treated. Baseball's ruling executive council found Cincinnati Reds' owner, Marge "Pay nigger, Say nigger" Schott, guilty of being one of them—white. The fact that Marge Schott frequently refers to Black athletes as "niggers," "damn nigger," and "dumb, lazy nigger" is nothing new to the world of corporate America. The fact that she got "caught" is something new. The fact that Major League Baseball only suspended her for one year, with reinstatement as soon as November 1, and let her maintain full ownership rights is nothing new. The fact that I still see brothas wearing Cincinnati Reds baseball caps is nothing new—but it's very sad.

What is happening in baseball is very similar to what is going on across the country. The racial bigotry expressed toward Blacks is extremely blatant. More and more, white society is getting away with slapping us in the face while they slap themselves on the wrist. The Marge Schott ruling is but a small incident that reflects the continous treatment which African Americans endure as we attempt to "function" in "the system." Yes, Pete Rose, George Steinbrenner, and Ted Turner have all been reprimanded for their faulty actions in the game, but none of them have gotten caught expressing their true feelings about the Black athlete and Black people in general. Al Campanis, on the other hand, did get caught—but...has his banishment had any effect on how white society treats Blacks, especially since Schott got away with what she did?

Once again, Black America is faced with owning up to Amerikkka's rhetoric. Case in point: everybody is focusing on the language used by Schott, but nobody (especially other baseball owners) is concerned with the mind-set of the white individuals who run baseball and their perceptions of the "colored" individual involved in the game. Is this Texaco or what?? We can't afford to let baseball (or any other sport, business, or organization) continue to get away with white-collar slavery that carries a million dollar price tag. The white individual knows that both sports and entertainment have become symbols of slavery for the African American. Sadly, they have both become our limited hopes for survival. This must stop. The fact that the owner of a major organization can get away with referring to Blacks as "dumb, lazy niggers" and saying "Hitler had the right idea" is sick because NOTHING IS BEING DONE TO STOP IT. Let Magic Johnson purchase a basketball franchise, hire white folks to play for him, and make them call him "Master." HA! Then, AIDS would be the least of his worries. And that's for real.

The Al Campanis-turned-Jimmy The Greek-turned Marge Schott syndrome will only continue if we fail to exercise our total power and demand BLACK RESPECT. And then maybe, just maybe, we will be able to give other baseball owners what they really deserve—A New Jack Swing.

NOTHIN' BUT LOVE

Ten years ago, a child lost the right to be the best. Chicago's Simeon High School basketball star, Ben Wilson, was struck down by one of the nameless bullets that have taken the lives of so many young African Americans.

This holiday season marks the 10th anniversary of Ben's death. Before he died, he was rated the No.1 high school basketball player in the nation. Today, "Benji" has become a symbol of young Black potential unfulfilled, a martyr for the thousands of youths whose lives have been cut short by this country's obsession with violence.

What made Benji different was not his ability to "rain" jump shots from 30 feet or do impressions of Magic Johnson, it was his character and his ability to remain humble in a life where success breeds neglect and irresponsibility. Unlike the athletes of today, Benji respected the game he played. At the same time, he never once flaunted what he had become, the best. He is, to this day, the only high school basketball player from Chicago ever to be recognized as the country's No. 1 player. But being No.1 never made him forget that he still had a mother to look up to. And despite winning the state championship his junior year, he never stopped sitting at the front of the CTA buses, listening to advice from old bus drivers who thought they knew more about basketball than he did. Despite being heavily recruited by top universities, he never forgot to give homeless and other less fortunate people in his neighborhood shoes when they needed them. At the age of seventeen, Benji was doing the things many of today's superstars are supposed to be doing, but without the $75 million contract.

Ben Wilson should have been recognized as our Michael Jordan without the gambling, our Magic Johnson without the infection, our Mike Tyson without Don King. The fact that he is not alive has little to do with him not receiving this recognition. In this day where a Black athlete's image supercedes his ability to create, it would be too much like right to uplift a young brotha who was more like Dr. King than Rodney King.

Humility. Some people can never find it. Chicago has never been a city that has thrived on that particular characteristic. Because of this, Chicagoans knew about Benji's basketball skills, but never knew the type of person he was. Nobody asked. The city was more concerned about his outside notoriety than his inner- prosperity. Here is a kid who had impeccable leadership qualities, strong family beliefs, and even demanded that his child (Benji had a two-month old son) be given his last name. But the city believed his scoring 25 points or grabbing ten rebounds was more important. You come to ask yourself, what's love got to do with anything?

So instead of being a role model, Benji became a victim. His life became a symbol of what to look out for instead of what to become. Neglect has set in. Gang symbols have been painted over a mural that sports Benji's name. The city refused to help Benji's mother raise money for a more appropriate headstone for his grave. The Jesse Jacksons, Nick Andersons, and city councilmen, who were once so concerned about Mary Wilson, are not as responsive to her telephone calls as they were when she was important to the media. This is the true Chicago hoop dream.

Now, Benji is the poster child for senseless violence. In a city where babies are thrown from high-rise rooftops or shot in the head execution style, the one Black person who could have been an example for the younger generation is only recognized when someone else dies too soon.

Yes, Benji was nice on and off the court. He played the game like George Gervin—smooth. He handled himself like Julius Erving—with class. He was a kid with a gift. He had a love which he shared with both basketball and mankind. He made you feel glad to be alive. He gave young African Americans who had lost all hope a reason to believe. The sad part is that he was never given a real chance to spread that love. A beautiful brotha that was taken away too soon. Damn.

Benji didn't deserve the fate or the neglect that continues to haunt him. He is one of the few people I'd love to trade places with right now, because he had the capability to do more with his life than I probably ever will. After ten years, somebody needs to understand what he truly stood for.

Mission Impossible: *The Source*, February 1995; Schott: *Rap Pages*, September 1993; Nothin' But Love: *Chicao Tribune*, November 21, 1994

Deion and Deion, Penny and Shaq

Don't Sweat
The Technique

"If you live my life, you'll be fighting to live." A deep line for a deep brotha. Many people go through life fighting for compassion, fighting for reason, fighting for understanding. Most fail. The words "if only they understood" pound in their heads like Chinese water torture.

A man is often measured by his image; image is everything. The clothes, the cars, the fly gold chains. For far too many, image outweighs a man's words and deeds, or even what is in a man's heart. If only they understood.

Professional athletics, a place where dreams meet reality and prodigies meet corruption. It is a place where there is little understanding. In this field of screams rests the American hero, the professional athlete—honored, revered, idolized, but rarely understood.

Deion Sanders is the most misunderstood of them all. Hidden behind the public's misperception is a hardworking Black man with a conscious, a devoted husband and a father of two. A man who does not curse, drink, or smoke, and who prefers fishing to hangin' out and livin' large.

He is a man with the ability to master. Even the

best of the best—Jordan, Ali, Gretsky, Ruth—could only do it in one sport. Deion's on another level. Two sports, football to baseball and back. From Pro Bowl to the World Series. Never resting. Sweat the technique. It's unreal. Understand?

Cincinnati, Slowhio. Home of WKRP and "a group of young men" (for you P-Funk fans). The Cincinnati Reds are at the top of their division and on top of the baseball world...well, what's left of it. The minute that I step onto the field, I see Deion swingin'. Practice makes perfect. There's so much flavor in the swing that you can sip it. How does a man go from pads to bats so effortlessly—professionally—with so much flavor? He turns around, drippin'. Bat in hand, he speaks.

"You know we can't do this now. YOU KNOW. You know I can't talk about football now. Especially when I'm not playing. You got to go through my people for that. I've got to concentrate on one thing at a time."

I understand. He knows that I know this, but you can't fault a brotha for trying. He doesn't. I give him the recital, "My bad." He responds.

"Naw it's cool, just not now. Let's do it later, in the future. I promise." His word is bond. We pound. I follow him into the locker room. Just us. Twenty-one pairs of Nikes are nestled at the bottom of his locker, a Luis Vuitton bag sits on his chair. Flavor. As he walks away, I notice the 8 1/2" by 11" sign hanging on the bay above his uniform: NO FOOTBALL QUESTIONS! LOVE. PEACE, 21.

To understand his brilliance, one must understand the man. The problem is, nobody does. He has built a "bafoon-style" smoke screen that gives him room to breathe. Behind this screen is where Deion lives, where no one can see. As the world continues to fall for this facade, Deion Sanders continues to get his. He grows, studies, and learns—more importantly, he excels. Nobody notices, nobody understands. How can a man continue to improve statistically, physically, and mentally at two sports every year for six years? He works. Oh, does he work. People have died so that he can do what he does. He says this, but nobody hears him. The smoke screen is too thick. So he moves on, ruling the NFL and mastering MLB. He's waiting for everybody else to catch on. They're asleep. He's awake.

"I think tradition states that you would have (a certain amount of) acclaim," he rightfully says. "And I may not. I think since I play baseball, I will never receive the credit for what I do. To come off the baseball field and get seven interceptions in eleven games—it's unbelievable to do that. Football is straight-out ability. Football is physical—strength and instinct. Baseball is mental. Big difference, man. You can't master baseball, you can just learn more about it. That's why there are so many damn alcoholics in baseball."

Instinct. His grid iron critics scream that he can't hit, that he's not Ronnie Lott. They, like everybody else, don't understand. Ronnie Lott was never voted NFL Defensive Player of the Year. Ronnie Lott never intercepted six passes in a season, turning half of them into touchdowns. Ronnie Lott never made offenses re-evaluate their entire game plan to avoid confronting him. Ronnie Lott scared players, Deion scares teams.

Deion is so dominating that he is often bored on the football field. The Chicago Bears, who were scared, "most definitely" bored him in last year's playoffs. Never testing him, never throwing in his direction because they feared what might happen. They cut the field in half and gave it to Deion.

"He's so fast," said Deion's cornerback partner on the 49ers, Eric Davis. "He's just like everybody in that he makes mistakes here and there, but his speed makes up for everything. He can take all of those chances you tell every defensive back not to do, but he's so fast—he has that luxury."

"He's without a doubt the most gifted athlete we'll ever see in this lifetime," says Air Force lieutenant and former professional baseball player, Andrew Brown. "People have no idea how hard it is for one man to play two sports professionally, at the same time, and be recognized as one of the best in both. No human being is supposed to be able to do that, not with the competition that's out there now."

"I work hard all week," Deion's voice begins to rise. "I pour my guts out everytime I'm on the field. Yes, I want it all. I come out of the huddle, as soon as I come off the ball, I'm thinking touchdown. I'm not a hard hitter. I feel I'm too valuable to my team to get out there and knock heads every minute. No. I think of myself as a big-play person. Fourth quarter. Prime time."

Few see Deion's commitment; it's shielded by the smoke screens. The media never talks about it, instead, they consider it a joke. When, in 1992, he played two games in one day, the media and society-at-large proclaimed it a stunt, a publicity thing. Can't a brotha just want to help his teams win? Nobody gets it.

Deion Sanders is a better football player than he is a baseball player. That's fact. He has the ability to change the complexion of every football game he plays. His presence scares quarterbacks, wide receivers, and coaches. Even though he's a solid .300 hitter, no baseball team is going to pitch around him the way football teams pass away from him.

He has an extra love for football. "In the hood, there's something about baseball that's not (hard) enough," he says. His agility and intensity, combined with the 4.1 speed, is unmatched in a league that considers Rod Woodson the apex. He excels in football because he has something to prove. His challenge is against other players, not the game.

"Football is more about doing your own thing," Deion says as he breaks down the aesthetics. "Baseball sets you up for failure. The game is always playing with you. You fail seven out of ten times (at bat) and you hit .300. That's good. Let me drop seven out of ten punts..."

He's finishing what Bo Jackson started and what Michael Jordan thought. Deion is taking everything to the next level. Everyday, his legend grows. From his days at North Fort Myers High School where he starred in track, football (quarterback, no doubt), baseball, and basketball. From his Florida State days where he received the Jim Thorpe Award as college football's best defensive back, played in the 1987 College World Series, and was an All-American in track, qualifying for the 1988 Olympics. He was drafted out of high school by the Kansas City Royals, ahead of Mark Grace, John Smoltz, and (cough, irony-irony) Bo Jackson. In the NFL, he was last year's defensive MVP and he was selected to the Pro Bowl four years running.

September 1994, Deion Sanders' life would change forever. People were still trippin' over the comments Deion had made last month in a *Playboy* magazine interview. From painting the "White House Black," to claiming "God is Black," to calling Spike Lee "a houseboy," to telling the white reporter, "I know what you think when you see me. When you're at a red light and I pull up in my Benz, the first thing you think, 'He's probably in drugs.'"

Weeks later baseball goes on strike, giving Deion the opportunity to play football full-time. Here he was, the best damn cornerback in the world, solo, unrestricted—a free agent. The Miami Dolphins floated a shallow offer, the New Orleans Saints prayed, the Detroit Lions roared, but it was the San Francisco 49ers who came up with the gold—a mill for one year, with a chance to win a ring.

"(Coach Seifer) damn near ran me away from here," Deion reminisced about the signing period with the 49ers. "It wasn't a pleasant meeting. I was pissed off after the meeting to be honest. That wasn't the time in my life I wanted to hear that crap." Crap about the smoke screen; believing that he's a joke, believing that he's not committed, believing that he's Neon instead of Deion. He continues, "If they had done their homework, they wouldn't have had (their original) assessment of me." But Deion's a business man for life. He put the personal bullshit aside, took the offer, made the 49ers look like fools and geniuses at the same time, and moved his heart to San Francisco—but he didn't leave it there.

He learned and so did they. "There's a hell of a difference between (SF) and Atlanta. The Niners didn't want to get to the Super Bowl—they wanted to win it." They did—easily. They overcame a Dallas arsenal that had Prime Time written all over it.

Michael Irvin, the Cowboy's All-World, second-to-Rice wide receiver, ate Frisco alive for two years in a row enroute to doubling-up on Super Bowl rings. The 49ers paid Deion $1 Million to stop this. One Mill, for one game—the rest of the season was irrelevant. "I came here to play in Miami," Deion boasted. The 49ers knew that the only way to get there was to neutralize Dallas, especially Irvin.

Bump & Grind, and a missed pass interference call—nobody saw anything wrong. Deion's and Michael's "classic" one play confrontation in the second quarter of that NFC championship changed the game, changed destiny.

"Yeah, Deion got me," Irvin would tell ESPN. "But that's part of the game. We'll laugh about it at the Pro Bowl."

After taking Dallas out, the 49ers traveled to Miami where they thoroughly massacred the San Diego Chargers. And while Steve Young and Jerry Rice got the glory and the SI commercial, those who understand football know. Twenty-one flavors, baby. Number 21...flavors.

It's hot, about 96 degrees in the shade. While Ron Gant, Barry Larkin, and Barry Bonds get taped-up 3 1/2 hours before the game starts, Deion Sanders is holding a private session with his bat. He strokes one deep into right field. Then another. The swing—although full of flavor—seems effortless. But you know it ain't. Too much hard work has gone into this for it to be natural. Yet, it never looks forced or mechanic. Smack! Line drive, left field. His eye contact with the ball is uncanny. Strength and instinct, this is baseball.

"Damn he's fine," says one female reporter, sweatin' it. She doesn't get it. More voices. "Incredible!" "Look at those arms, like, like... a horse." "Why does he have to wear his hair like that?" Another one, lost. People see the smoke screen and fall for it. The gold, the flare, the nicknames, the Nikes. Because he's so outspoken, he's not heard. Because he is not shallow, he is not understood.

They don't understand that this man did more in his first week in Cincinnati for minority youth than any of his Reds teammates who had been there for years. They don't understand his consciousness: a Black superstar with a Black agent. No, they don't understand. He'll say Bo Jackson "inspired" him and he'll give 49ers defensive coach Ray Rhodes all of the credit for his defensive MVP last year. Giving too much credit where fractional credit is due, it's a Deion thing. Nobody understands.

"If you live my life you'll be fighting to live." A deep line for a deep brotha. Life has never experienced a Deion Sanders before. Yeah Michael, Wayne, Carl, Willie, Muhammad, and Babe all represented well, but none quite like this. Deion is the definition of the modern sports era. He defines the post-soul sports culture credited to Ken Griffey, Jr. and Grant Hill. He defines ghetto heaven. He's only 28.

Deion pauses. It's a long pause. He surrenders. "I just see myself as someone who's blessed. They don't understand." As he runs, defends, intercepts, and high-steps, embarrassing opposing teams and white-collar organizations, he crams for understanding. With each swing and stolen base, he crams. With each punt return or reception, he wants us to understand his feelings along with his flavor. He has so much to give. Is it too much for us to accept? Don't you understand?

A Love Supreme

Memphis, Tennessee, the home of Beale Street and Dr. King's death. Growing up down south has a special kind of vibe for young Black kids who dream of owning their own land instead of visiting Graceland. Pride and humbleness, along with an appreciation for life, run deep down here. Brothas who are raised in the nucleus of the Civil Rights Movement reserve the right to be human—and there ain't nothin' civil about that.

Anfernee Hardaway is a product of that movement. Twenty-three-years-old, strong with pride and humble with appreciation, he has done nothing less than reserve the right to be a man, his own man, a blessed man whose face belongs on a copper coin.

To appreciate this young man's game, you have to study history—marches, sit-ins, protests, beat downs, water hoses, and German Shepards. When you live down south, you carry a scar to remind you about all that was done for you to survive, live a normal life, and play ball.

Penny has that scar. He doesn't display it or flaunt it like Larry Johnson's gold tooth. He keeps it in his heart—somewhere close so that he can reach it anytime life in the NBA gets off the hook. Yes, he is calm, cool, and too collected, but he is also scarred.

He's not supposed to be here. History doesn't support it. Long not tall, skinny not boney, Anfernee Hardaway is not supposed to carry the weight Oscar Robinson and Earvin Johnson left behind. Real ball players come from larger, well-respected places like New York, Detroit, Chicago, DC, and Baltimore. You know, concrete jungles. A young brotha from Memphis with game? Oh, but no. The city already banked everything on Keith Lee in the '80's. Bankrupt. Memphis' total investment in the NBA went pop like Brandy. Baby, baby, baby. See, Lee didn't struggle. Things were made too easy for him. He wasn't part of the civil rights. No CORE, no SNCC, no spine. He had no scar.

Not Penny. He tore up the league as a rookie, started in an NBA All-Star game, was selected to the NBA All-First Team, and played in the NBA Finals. New jack or reincarnation? A 6'7" Marcus Haynes with a jumper. George Gervin with hoops. Bob Cousy with color and a scoring average. Copper coin. Relax. Analyze the game, so sweet. Find the scar, so deep. The comparisons with Magic and Big O come in droves. All three have ugly post-up games with dangerous turn-around jumpers. The dimes and handles reflect the Magic in him, while the defense, rebounding, and scoring bring out the Oscar in him. But neither "O" nor "E" had a jump shot like Penny, nor did they have his range; and neither one of them had his ups. He's probably the only point guard in the league that people get excited to see on a break away. Earl Monroe with David Thompson's jumping ability, he breaks defenders down like syllables, leaves them stranded like Gilligan, only to finish off the fool-for-a-center who thinks he can block the party.

Always with grace, always in your face. Penny embarrasses people on the court with style. Southern hospitality, thought you knew. The Knicks know. Last season they were the victims of one of those moments that define players' careers. Penny's dunk on Patrick Ewing was one of those moments.

Orlando, Florida. Magicville. No civil rights. Anfernee Hardaway gets flipped around on draft day and winds up on the south coast. Shaquille O'Neal is already there, Chris Webber was slated to be there. Once the script got flipped, Penny heard the boos in Orlando. Appreciation, not everyone has it.

"When I was about 7 or 8-years-old," says Penny, "I kinda realized that this was what I wanted to do. I played football and baseball, but for some reason I liked basketball the best. The sun on the baseball field stopped me from doing that, and my grandmother felt I was too small to really play football, so... But still to this day, I can honestly tell you that I need to work on my game. Everything! That's just the type of person I am. Free throw shooting, jump shot, and defense. I think that I can really do better in those areas. The things that come naturally— I'm thankful for, but there's still work to be done.

"The comparisons to Magic keep me humble, but they don't put pressure on me to play that way. When Magic says, 'looking at him play is like looking in a mirror,' that only makes me work harder. I'll admit that maybe, maybe, I can do some things that make people think of him, but there'll only be one Magic."

Deeper. How has your friendship with Magic

helped that?

"It has helped a lot because I hear the things I need to hear from him. Like when I'm playing well he'll call me and tell me, and when I'm playing bad he'll tell me what's going on. He and Oscar have rings, it's that simle."

The 1995 NBA Finals. Anfernee Hardaway, point guard extraordinaire and new school hoop legend, led a once playoff-drought Orlando squad to the show. Not physically healthy at the end of the season, Penny worked every bit of his talent to get back into the groove. And although the Magic got mopped 4-zip by the Rockets, Penny proved, once again, that he was the future of the Orlando Magic organization—and the NBA.

Now, everybody on the Orlando roster has a scar. They've witnessed defeat up-close, personally. Nick gets the ill Bill Buckner treatment for missing four "dollars" at the line in Game one. Look deeper. Early on in the first quarter, while the Magic were building their ground-breaking 20-point lead (which turned out to be the last significant lead they had in the series), Penny over-zealously reacted after a couple of dunks. Usually cool like Heathcliff, he "uncharacteristically" showed his emotions. The clenched fist. The yell. The indirect "we're about to run y'all" behavior. It lasted less than 10 seconds. Too long, too late.

"That really wasn't me," Penny says. Even though he has been known to "irritate" some players in the league by talkin', showin', and provin', he never disrespects any player or any team; he's not Reggie Miller. His "reaction" did something to Houston though, because the series was never the same afterwards. "Once they see you react, they have you. In the league you can never let them see you sweat. I have to keep that in mind at all times.

"We know we were a lot better than we showed (in the finals). The mental strain of losing drains you. It makes you angry because you're not promised to get (to the finals), that's why (losing) was so disappointing. The only emotion for us was disbelief. I still don't think they are four games better than us.

"We watched them celebrate. That was our motivating factor to come back next year." As he speaks, you can see him refrain from getting deeper. Never again will he expose the emotions, the scar. Remember, civil rights "leaders" don't preach, they march. March to prove a point, prove that they belong. Magic and Oscar got theirs, don't think Penny's marching to the beat of a different drummer.

Take me to another place. Take me to another land. Make me forget all that hurts me. Let me understand the plan. On July 15th, Penny's plan was to come home to give his people what they wanted, more importantly, what they needed. Summer b-ball. A charity sanctioned game during the NBA lock-out summer. Contracts and insurance policies out the window, a collection of NBA players came together under the groove to show their skills, to show their love for a brotha who plays like Magic and wears Oscar's number.

"Believe it or not, Memphis is a big basketball city," Penny stresses. I shoulda asked somebody. "The city deserves this. Just to be able to bring their favorite basketball players here to see them play in person, is special."

Scottie Pippen, John Starks, and Robert Horry show up. Cedric Ceballos, Nick "I Can Out Shoot The

World" Van Exel, and Juwan Howard also come through. Memphis heroes Todd Day and Elliot Perry represent the hometown. And of course, winter teammates Nick Anderson and Dennis "3D" Scott bring love. Shawn Kemp was on the roster but wasn't able to make it. Grant Hill had "fila" problems; And Shaq? Many questions, no answers. Penny's show must go on. Pippen tosses the rock off the glass on a fast break (in traffic!) for a catch 'n cup from-the-foul line dunk, Van Exel hits 7 threes in a row and Cedric Ceballos scores 60, but who's counting. Game over, mad fun had by all. The prodigal son tosses in 47 of his own, and his team wins.

He has probably only played better and had more fun once, in Scottie Pippen's Summer Classic last year when Jordan scored 52. People don't know this, but Penny actually outplayed Jordan that night, easily. He scored 42 and had almost about 80 assists. This type of ball was made for him to play: open-court, freestyle, no-pay basketball. Other players whisper about his skills, but he never hears it.

"He's so fluent in his game," says John Starks, "Very rarely do you see someone at 6'7" do what he can do."

"He has moves only I can dream about," says Todd Day, who rarely gives anyone credit.

Even the point guard who Penny feels is the best in the league comes clean. "His future is so bright, it's unbelievable," Kevin Johnson reluctantly says because he and Penny caught beef earlier last year in a pre-season game. "I'll give him all the credit he deserves. You watch him play, and you can't imagine a guy having this much ability and being only in his second year in the league."

Starks keeps rollin'. "What do I hate about gaurding him? His post up game. Plus he has that turn-around. I put him in the Magic Johnson mode, nice, huh?"

Ultra nice. In his game and fame, he remains the same. Sweat the Nike commercials, too cool. Clyde Frazier, the sequel. He speaks only when spoken to, is silent on "ignorant" media questions, and has no problems emphasizing how hard he had to work to get where he is. "No silver spoons," he says. The southern Memphis-fried character that was instilled in him by his grandmoms still influences his every emotion—every feeling.

"When I was young, I used to see my dreams through the older guys I played against." Penny is introspective for a second, then it's back to chill mode. "Like now, playing with Travis and all of the other young guys. They can see their dreams through me by playing me in one-on-ones, or two-on-twos. "I'm still living out my dream. Everytime I go out on the court I'm living that dream, thanking God in my head all of the time. Will basketball define my life? I really don't know. I've been blessed. I've been doing this all of my life, and (all of a sudden) I'm getting paid millions to do this..." He smiles, "...whatta you think? I'm blessed."

He travels around Memphis like a demi-god—like a Black Elvis. You cannot find one person in the city to say one bad word about him. It's a horrible angelic feeling that only Grant Hill knows. A love supreme. It's also a sign of being truly blessed. It is much more difficult to achieve this "in-house" love than it is to win an NBA championship. Think I'm wrong, ask Houston. Two rings, no love.

The Large Professor:

Inside The Black Future of Shaquille O'Neal

haquille O'Neal is large. He commands space and he demands attention. He has rhyme skillz that are certified gold, and he has acheived blue chip status at the box office. For Reebok, he's paid. For Pepsi, he's paid. In two years, Shaquille O'Neal has gone from phenom to icon. He has redefined the American mythology of superstardom. Never has a young Black man (with the exception of Eddie Murphy) gained such a vast amount of fame in such a short amount of time. Rule: Be young, have fun—be Shaq.

You never really know the magnitude of Shaq until you have to interview him. We hooked up at the World Basketball Championship practice facilities in Chicago. I was told that I had 30 minutes and Shaq knew I was coming. Cool. I walked in and spotted largeness.

"Yo, what up?"

"Wassup."

"Heard you're down for the interview."

"Yeah, let's hook up after I go to the pool and stretch out."

"Cool."

"Peace."

"Peace."

It took Shaq three weeks to get out of the pool.

Over the past four years, I've had the fortune of meeting and interviewing a number of high profile people: Spike Lee, Tom Cruise, Magic Johnson, Eddie Murphy, Chuck D., Mike Tyson, Charles Barkley, Elvis...just joking. But never have I experienced anything like my interview with Shaq. His life is madness. From Chicago to Charlotte back to Chicago to Michigan back to Chicago to Oakland to Toronto. Chasing him was like trying to find Jimmy Hoffa. But I learned.

I learned that Shaquille O'Neal means a lot of things to a lot of people. They live for his services, his appearances, and his smile. Kids run to him like he's Michael Jackson. Adults flock to him like he's the 8th Wonder of the world. Hoop fans sweat him like he's the next...(should I say it?) Jordan. It seems unfair that a 22 year-old kid has to handle this. His family and a couple of his boys absorb some of the chaos. But damn, it's honestly too much demand, too much pressure, too much nonsense. Will he ever be "the man?" Yes, we all know that he is "the man" in various annals, but not in basketball. Not yet. He wrecked the league last year with MVP numbers (29.3 PPG-second in the league, 13.2 RPG-second in the league, 60% FGP-first in the league, and 231 BLKS-sixth in the league), but nobody seemed to care. Basketball is this kid's life, yet society and the powers- that-be let his "versatility" overshadow the reality that this might be one of the most gifted athletes ever. He's what Darryl Dawkins was supposed to be, what Chris Washburn needed to be, what Moses Malone used to be. But somehow we've all forgotten that.

The question is, has he? With all of the outside activities and all of the preoccupied notoriety, I decided I'd ask him something different. With all of the magazine covers, the questions about his side-burns, and who he "kicks it" with, I figured I'd throw this big AllSport drinkin' brotha a curve. With all of these unconcerned journalists, advertising agents, and business executives asking Mr. O'Neal about product endorsements, I thought I'd ask Shaq about the one area of his life that nobody else seems to be interested in. I asked Shaq about basketball. "It's about time."

SCOOP: What place does basketball have in your life right now?
SHAQ: "Right now, it's the most important thing. Everything else comes second. Because without basketball, I wouldn't have any of these other things anyway."

What's the difference in your game now as compared to three years ago?
"My skills have become sharper, as well as my knowledge of the game."

Since you've been in the NBA, has the game become easier for you or more difficult?
"Easier. Because in college they can play zone, but in the NBA we play one-on-one. I just hate zone defenses."

Where do you feel you can dominate most effectively,

on offense or defense?
"Both. It really just depends on the game situation. I can dominate on the offense and defense..."

What about when "blonde ambition" (Dennis Rodman) held you scoreless in the last quarter of that game against San Antonio?
"I just didn't have the ball enough at the end of the game—and it's hard to score without it."

Is he that good defensively, or did you just have a bad quarter?
"Dennis is definitely one of the best defensive players, but..."

Where do you feel you have room for improvement in your game?
"On the free throw line. But there's always room for improvement in everybody's all-around game."

How hard was it for you to adjust to the defense (and defensive strategies) in the NBA?
"It's something that every rookie has to go through, I was no exception. But it all gets better with time."

What do you feel separates you—skill wise—from Hakeem, Patrick, and David?
"I think I'm more of a power player. My game is in the paint."

Last year was a very strange year for the Big Brotha. 1994, as George Orwell so convincingly predicted, would be a "special" year, or season for those who engage. The Orlando Magic went to the playoffs for the first time in franchise history. Expectations were high. Anfernee Hardaway surpassed all expectations. The rest of the squad, however, were not ready for prime time. Basketball is a sport where individuals— not the team, coaches, or the front office—take the blame. If you don't believe it, ask John Starks. Shaq took the heat.

Explain what happened to the Magic in the playoffs.
"We just got beat by a great Indiana team. But trust me, it won't happen again this year."

What do you think the Magic needs to do to win a championship?
"Well we got Horace Grant (from the Chicago Bulls) this year, and that definitely will help. The team just needs to stick together."

You've had the fortune of playing with two of the best guards ever. How would you rate Chris (Mamute Abdul-Rauf, point guard at LSU) and Penny (Anfernee Hardaway, point guard for the Orlando Magic) after playing only one year with both?
"They are both great point guards. Chris is a little more offensively minded, but both can make incredible dishes (passes). I'm lucky."

Along with point guards come coaches. A true assessment of any ball career can be traced by listening to the people who coached the player. In this case, Shaq is special. He's a basketball coach's dream. Hell, he's a football and WWF coach's dream too. This is where players don't get credit for being productive. It becomes a mind game, a Pat Riley thang. Shaq has dealt with three different coaches in three years. When you have the capability to "own" the sport you're playing, it's very hard to listen to someone who is not busting their ass out there taking elbows from Bill Cartwright. Shaq is on another level though, and ain't too many coaches going to check the uncheckable.

"There really isn't a center out there that is going to match up with him one on one," says Orlando Magic Head Coach Brian Hill, who knows a meal ticket when he coaches one. "He's a little more than a dunker. (Although) he does have a lot of dunks, he scores about every way imaginable with short jump shots, turnarounds, jump hooks and everything else. You watch him every night, you tend to take him for granted. What can I say? He's triple-teamed everytime he catches the ball down low. (Still) he either makes his move to the basket or he plays like a team player and throws the ball out to an open player so they can get their shots. In my mind there's only one MVP in this league and that's Shaquille O'Neal."

You'd never hear that from Bobby Knight.

During the World Championships (three weeks after we met in Chicago), Shaquille proved that he is among the best in the world. He led Dream Team II in scoring (18ppg), rebounding (8.6), and field-goal percentage (76%). "I'm happy for myself, my family, and my friends to have been on Dream Team II. All that really matters—and what I'll probably remember most about the tournament—is that we won the gold medal."

Have you gotten over not being on Dream Team I?
"Yeah. I was happy for Dream Team I."

How good is Alonzo Mourning?
"I've always respected Alonzo's game."

And including yourself, who do you think is the best ball player on the squad?
"I don't know, you'll have to ask the coach."

July, August, September—and it don't stop. Shaq took about four days off, played the ghost role, and then it was off to LA for a Reebok commercial shoot. Yo, Calgon take me away! How long will it last? They say a couple of days. I know better. Shaq knows better too. Away from basketball, but still on top of it. Shaq breaks down the rules:

"Training camp and pre-season is where I really get my conditioning. And during the off-season I try to eat right and work on my individual skills, so it's important. I don't feel that I have to prove myself to anybody, but the people I play against better respect me. I'd like to win a championship. Before I leave Orlando, I'll have a few."

Does it bother you when people question your intensity?
"No, because I know I play every game hard. I just don't worry about what other people say."

Everybody is talking about the style of play changing in the league. What are your feelings and do you feel your presence has anything to do with that?
"Man, I really don't think about all of that stuff. I just go out there to play hard. All these other things will take care of themselves."
Then I hit him with the bomb...

Have you ever wished you were a point guard? "Who says I'm not? I have a better handle than Isiah. The coach just won't let me show it (laugh)!" I expected him to say some shit like that.

After doing the "bi-coastal-intercontinental pool tour," I feel different. I feel honored, yet I feel concerned. I've watched too many people try to do too many things at the same time—and lose it all. I've watched the media and corporate companies build young Black athletes and entertainers into demigods, only to watch them fall. In the hood, we call it a damn shame.

In Chicago, Shaq told me that hookin' up was going to be tough. But, "I won't let you down," he promised. Brotha to brotha, I trusted him. And it's always the ones you trust who you seem to worry about the most. Shaq's like that. He's the future of a new generation—but not just those who drink Pepsi. He seems focused and centered, rare for a brotha only 22 years of age. After two years in the league, dealing with all of the outside projects, media b.s., and business endeavors, basketball is still his life...and he knows it.

"I love the game," he screams. No joke? "Man, I'd play for free!"

I told you he was large.

Deion: *Blitz*, March 1995; Penny: *Slam*, September 1995; Shaq: *Slam*, November 1994

Channel Zero

Yhitewater

Black man sees five Black kids on the corner, he sees trouble. A white man sees five Black kids on the corner, he sees money. That's what separates. A racially specific look at how things really are only widens the gap nobody seems to want to close. Give me a beat.

Beat given. Once again, theft breeds some other type of contempt. See, those five "niggas" on the corner got skills, mad ones. They wreck bodies and turn parties out, soon to get an article in *Rappages*, maybe *VIBE*, or *The Source*. Even *RapSheet* might notice them. There they are, posing in the pages along-side Hev. D., KRS, and Biggie with Death Row covers and 4-mic ratings. Yeah kid, you large. Or at least that's what we thought...

In the confines of hiphop, these publications—the ones that mean so much, have become our "bibles," our only national source of information on the rap scene—all but one *(RapSheet)* owned by the man who knows that dollars, not sense, keeps Black kids in trouble, but will make him rich. Welcome to Yhitewater. A place where grown white men publish magazines about young Black culture; the same Black culture they depise and the same music they "fear" their children will hear.

Nothing is Black-owned here. For Yhitewater has a way of keepin' it real...Amerikkkan.

Ain't nothin' new. Since hiphop's inception, Yhitewater has existed in record companies, lawyers, and concert promoters, the whole nine-mm. "Def Comedy Jam" is owned by HBO, not BET. But literature remains a more sacred form of exploitation than MTV or Tommy Boy. Through "the big three" (*VIBE, The Source, and Rappages*), we are given guidelines into a world we created, but no longer control.

Now, there is nothing wrong with somebody going for theirs (regardless of color), but...since hiphop is the last Black mecca of creativity left in this country, it seems like there should be some sorta culture-controlled publication that is true to the very essence of the life about which we rhyme. From Dave Mays to John Rollins to Larry Flynt, the Yhitewater network keeps the pages flowin' with Blackness, while Kevin Powell, Dream Hampton, Sheena Lester, and Adario Strange play big Willie-style on the edit screen, lookin' for the next George Nelson, Cheo Coker, or Bonz Malone. And you thought that the whitepages was a telephone directory? Artist after artist breaks down the magazine's doors just to get a rep, or at least a dope photo shoot. Reader after reader subscribes like a crack fiend, never able to wait for next month's issue because—it's "gonna be the bomb." Believe the hype, there is no sequel.

The Source is large. No doubt Dave Mays knew what he was doing when he decided to write about a culture that "fascinated" him in the early 80's. His conventional wisdom gave Black people a line of hope that "this hiphop shit is serious." It was serious business, serious money, a magazine for the future, a hiphop

Rolling Stone. Bam! Other "biznessiz" saw the profit, saw the demand, saw those five "niggas" on the corner, and went to work. Invasion.

The beat might drop, but not like all the others... Somehow, someway, this has to change. Due to the fact that these magazines are so important to the hiphop information highway, it is imperative that something Black get a piece of that pie, or at least a publisher's page. Through ingenious financial backing (or some brotha with ends who believes that five Black kids on a corner are worth investing in, instead of running from), the culture of hiphop can be reported with the true dignity it deserves.

The invasion is no joke. Never was, never will be. Watergate. Whitewater. Yhitewater. Conspiracy? Let's just say: When the Pillsbury Doughboy starts rhyming, beat noxin', selling b-boy crescent rolls, Quaker Oats makes big money and a "brotha" does not get a check at the end of the day for inventing that shit—something's seriously wrong!

Start. Props. The magazines of hiphop music, culture, and politics live on. And on and on and on, and it "won't" stop. Invasions never do. It ain't like *VIBE, Rappages,* and *The Source* got a lock on white magazines owning hiphop. *Spin* and *GQ* give up more ink to the culture than *Ebony* ever will. It's never about that. It's about preservation, preserving what is rightfully ours. The beat. It belongs to us, the brothas on the block from Queens to Compton, corner to corner, page to page. Five brothas on a corner, the choice is yours. 'Cause right now, all we got left is the beat.

Reality Check:
Menace or Not,
Here it Comes

Welcome to Black America. How are you livin'? Every now and then, Black America has to come to grips with its own rhetoric. First, it was rap music. Then it was Clarence Thomas and Mike Tyson, and most recently, the L.A. riots/revolutions. Now, there's the film *Menace II Society*. In the annals of the Black anthology, certain events will stand out for their influence on societal perceptions of Black life. *Menace II Society* is one of them.

The Hughes brothers, fascinated with being "down" instead of being Black, succeeded in doing something that white people have been trying to do for centuries: Tell you that Black life has no hope. No future. No purpose.

In the history of cinema, no film has actually changed Black life or lifestyle. Even in the critically acclaimed, *Do The Right Thing*, there weren't too many short Black kids in Brooklyn Dodger's jerseys throwing trash cans through store front windows (even though the killing of Black citizens by police officers did increase, go figure). Menace...is no different. The film is strictly a mirror image of some life in the hood. A sad image, but an image.

Based on the sad realities of growing up broke and Black, *Menace II Society* strikes at the heart of any individual who is unaware of why some young Black men do the things we do. And unlike its father film (*Boyz 'N The Hood*), it leaves Black people uninformed and white people happy.

Movie critic Roger Ebert gladly gave the movie four stars. His partner in crime, Gene Siskel, threw his thumb way up in the air. The New York Times, the Boston Globe, and USA Today cherished the film. Michael Medved of "Sneak Previews" dubbed the movie "remarkable." Why? Because art is supposed to imitate life.

Black people have no control over the film industry, yet we glorify and justify everything that it produces. The powers-that-be have an even larger role in this game. Through all sorts of media, they control portions of the Black thought process, behavior activities, and destiny. *Menace II Society* is much more in line with "their" Black direction than ours.

If left up to white America the movie will make money. Probably much more than "*Malcolm X.*" Because of that, more movies like Menace will be made. What's the point in watching 110 minutes of senseless Black-on-Black genocide when you can simply watch the news every night?

Oh yeah, there are other problems, but why go there? Why talk about how movie critics discouraged audiences from seeing *Posse* because they did not like seeing white people getting killed by brothas on the big screen? Why talk about all of the other quality screenplays and scripts by African American writers that lay on the desks of Hollywood executives, never to be seen because they have "redeeming social value" and no destructive focus point? Why talk about how every brotha in the film, except for the most degenerate one (O-Dog played with brilliance by Larenz Tate), gets killed? Why talk about filmmakers who have no idea of what it is to "bang," but are quick to portray it just to get their start?

The "fifteen minutes of fame" theory is getting out of hand. The time has come to realize the importance of our ventures. As Black films gain popularity, they also gain importance. And as good a film as *Menace II Society* is, it is more important than it is good. Important, not because of its message (whatever that may be), but because of its lack of justification. There really is no need for it. Black people are doing too much to have our lives constantly portrayed in this way. Our situation is bad enough as it is. The last thing we need is an "exaggerated reality check" to keep us down. The news media does that for us for free. Now, thanks to the Hughes brothers, most of us are out $7.50 and out of our minds.

I WANT MY MTV?

Back in the summer of 1992, the other side got ill. There was a big riot during and after a Guns N' Roses/Metallica concert held in Montreal, Canada. Concession stands smashed, fires set, cars overturned—you know the whole 9. But did any of you hear about it? Doubt it. Why? Because according to white boys, rock doesn't cause ill behavior—only rap does that (Ha!).

Once again, here's the media determining the fate of our culture. Media reports of "rap violence" have made it almost impossible to put on a rap concert. But when shit happens on their end, the "other" end (at a rock concert), it's see, hear, and say no evil.

The white media continues to keep "slavery n' effek" by white-washing news concerning them while they over-expose and over-exaggerate negative news about us. How in the hell can whites blame rap groups like NWA, Ice T, Cube, and PE for inciting violence and not blame the movie *Home Alone* for white parent neglect? How can they not blame *Flatliners* for the increasing number of white teenagers committing suicide? How can Howard Stern appear on national tell-lie-vision & radio and show his ass (literally), but Flavor Flav is their idea of ignorance? Ya C Where I'm Comin' from?!?

Regardless of race, creed, color, or musical taste, when a bunch of people get together on a large scale, the chance of something jumping off is great. That's Murphy's Law. We also need to remember Media Law: Target Black life to expose society's ills. So, without getting too—Chuck D verbally, think about this: Who is our worst enemy, the cops or the media?

The Lost Boyz: OJ, Tupac, Arsenio and Tyson

JUICED!

The American Reality

"OJ's plane was late, so he had an hour to kill."

For some reason, this had to be written. There is a certain thing in life called, "The Black Truth." Now, it's vastly different from a "white lie." When telling The Black Truth, one has to appoint him or herself the bearer of bad news. The Black Truth hurts. It hurts to say it and it hurts to hear it. But the one thing that can be said about the Black Truth: It is always based on fact. That's more than can be said about a white lie.

The Black Truth is obvious. The Black Truth is that OJ Simpson shouldn't have been messing with the white woman in the first place—but we won't go there. The Black Truth is that OJ Simpson stopped being Black a loooong time ago—but we won't go there. The Black Truth is that there is a job opening at Hertz—but we won't go there either. The Black Truth is that too many Black children are being killed on a daily basis across this country to be overly concerned about the death of someone outside of "our" family. Here, we will go.

Since when did Nicole Brown become more important than LaTosha Harlings, Elenor Bumpus, Dantrell Davis, Michael Steward, Yusef Hawkins, Malice Green, James Jordan or any of the individuals being killed in Rwanda, South Africa or Haiti? The Black Truth is that we have an over-abundance of overkill in our own communities. We cannot be concerned with the media's overexposure of OJ. That's the Black Truth.

The OJ Simpson situation could not have been avoided—at least not in this country. Success and Black life connect where success and Black lifestyle do not meet. The American Dream does not allow it. OJ, Michael Jackson, Charles Barkley, Clarence Thomas, Bryant Gumbel, etc., all have taken total advantage of what Amerikkka has to offer. In the process of doing this, their "souls" got juiced. Just like Sunkist.

These "negroes" have found new lives to live, new things to buy, and new friends to keep. Their zip codes became unfamiliar, and their women became paler. It makes no difference what the profession; if the white man is going to pay the Black man big money, then the Black man is going to "hang" (pun intended) with the white man. The white man is going to show off the Black man as his new prize and the next time that the Black man looks up, he's surrounded by whiteness. White women, white suits, white Chevy Broncos.

OJ is a victim of living this Amerikkkan Dream, but he is not alone. Many African American celebrities believed the hype was real. Then, they found out what real was. Being accused of murdering two white people in this country is real. No Black man has ever lived after killing (or being accused of killing) any person void of melanin. That's the Black Truth.

The pulp is the soul of the Black man in this metaphoric tale of living a white lie. The white lie deceives you. Too often those individuals who are present for us, are removed from us, and are then strung-up to represent us. They become puppets, reminding us that, in "their" eyes, we are still niggers. Niggers with no juice.

The Black Truth is that maybe OJ would have been better off squeezing the trigger? Who knows? Because watching "them" squeeze the soul out of him brings our own souls closer to death. They tease us, then they squeeze us. Why? It has nothing to do with us, they just want the juice.

Once again, we have another brotha to tell our kids not to emulate."Don't be like OJ, son, because he may have murdered somebody." "Don't be like Michael Jackson, son, because he may have played with little children the wrong way." "Don't be like Clarence Thomas, son, because he verbally degrades and harasses women." The Black Truth is, don't be like any of these people, son, because they surrounded themselves with individuals who don't love them for being what they are: Black men.

JUST ANOTHER
BLACK MAN CAUGHT
UP IN THE MIX

Another stain on the sidewalk. It would be naive to say that we didn't know that Tupac was going to die too soon. Even he knew it. The death of Tupac Shakur again reminds us that Black society, regardless of notoriety or fame, has an alarming tendency to turn on itself faster than any law enforcement official ever could.

What made Tupac's death different from the other shootings that occur daily in hundreds of Black neighborhoods across the country was not the fact that Tupac was famous, but that it wasn't random. What makes this shooting similar to all of the other Black-on-Black crimes is the "expediency" in which the police catch the men that committed the crime.

Tupac Shakur was never one of America's sweethearts. He was the Mike Tyson of the entertainment industry. His outside activities—living the thug life—overshadowed the fact that he was a gifted rap artist and actor. His appearances in *Juice, Poetic Justice,* and

Above The Rim were spellbinding. His albums were classic. He had become Black America's un-focused prince and white America's nightmare. Many called him a time bomb waiting to explode; others called him a hero. Now we call him dead.

The Black James Dean. The one brotha that will be idolized for his defiance. Tupac represents the anger and passion felt by individuals who have no right to fight and no rights to fight for. Although many feel Tupac brought this on himself (including Alan Light, editor of VIBE), he is deservedly well-loved by those who understand the hell he went through to get the little bit of fame he received.

Through his words, Tupac made it clear that his main problem was living the life of a Black man. Nobody listened. Society never heard the brotha when he said he would be dead by the time he was twenty-five. Nobody cared that he damn-near raised himself after his mother got hooked on crack. Tragic life; tragic life style.

Even though he was large, he was just another Black man caught up in the mix, trying to survive. He's gone and gangsta livin', with its drive-by mentality, lives on. Damn, what did he really die for?

TURNABOUT DESERVES FAIR PLAY:
The Mike Tyson Ordeal:

"I'm Sorry. I realize that a few—if not a whole lotta—people (especially women) are going to be quite upset with me after they read this piece. But YO!, somebody's got to get Mike's back. So, at the risk of losing a few friends, I'm going to say some shit that needs to be said.

I'm Tired. For the last month I've watched everybody—and I do mean everybody—take shots at Mike Tyson. Immediately after the verdict was released, people used television, radio, and newspapers to discredit, disclaim, dishonor, and diss Mike Tyson—especially those Pat Buchanan-loving, Pat Sajak-watching white boys employed by CNN, ESPN, and all the other networks. The bottom line in every comment was that "Mike Tyson ain't shit, and we told you so!" Well—FK Y'ALL!

I'm Curious. Why aren't there different degrees of criminal charges pertaining to rape? You know, like in murder. There is first degree murder, second degree murder, third degree murder, manslaughter, and involuntary manslaughter. I realize that rape is rape, but at the same time, consideration needs to be given to circumstances, intent, and degree of proof. Example 1: A man with a knife breaks into a woman's home, beats and stabs her, ties her up and then rapes her. This sadistic bastard should be convicted of rape in the first degree and castrated. Example 2: A woman accepts a man's invitation to visit his hotel room after a dinner date. The next day, the woman tells police that after consentual foreplay, the man raped her. The man, however, claims that the sex was consentual. There were no witnesses: it's his word against hers. Should this man face the same charges as the sadist in example 1? I don't think so.

It is one thing to be evil; it is quite another to be stupid. Stupidity is not a crime. If it was, then both Tyson and Miss Beauty Pageant would have done some time. First, Miss Beauty Pageant shouldn't have agreed to come out of her room at 2 AM. She shouldn't have taken off her "shield" if she wasn't planning on doin' somethang. And she damn sure shouldn't have let Tyson go "downtown." At the same time, Mike should have just gone and bought a piece of ass and called it a day. I mean, with $50 million, you never let your "little head" do the thinking—you let your wallet!

I'm Disgusted. What's up with all the commentary about Mike Tyson's lack of character? It is true that Tyson didn't read Martha Stewart's lastest book or never made it to finishing school. It is also true that Mike Tyson never had a mother or father or grandparents or uncle or sister to teach him how to live. He grew up with nothing!

Here is a young man who was raised by the only person who befriended him as an adolescent. He grew up with one friend; and as soon as he gained fame and fortune, that friend, Cus D'Amoto, died. What in the hell is a 19 year-old, homeless, Black kid, with no education, no family, no friends, no foundation, and $50 million (legally!) supposed to do? The fact that Mike Tyson lived past the age of 21 is amazing in itself. I know grown men who could not have handled all the "stuff" Mike went through as a child without committing suicide, or having been a victim of homicide. How does a young man go from having females at Burger King reject him one day, to having fine, rich, famous Lisa Bonet-type women asking him out the next?!? Seriously, at 19 or 20 years old (with no family to discuss this with), what psychological effect does that have on a young man? We forget about the mental aspect when money is involved. Most people were sitting around thinking that Tyson was lucky because of his fast rise to fame and fortune. Wrong! Nothing in this American Dream comes easy.

I'm Pissed. The lack of racial solidarity between Black men and women is killing us. In the last few years, "Charlie" has had great success in encouraging sistahs to publicly sell out brothas for money. Who convinced Rasheeda Moore to trap Marion Berry? Who orchestrated the Anita Hill/Clarence Thomas affair? Who paid that bitch Ralph Abernathy to (try to) denounce Martin Luther King? Who forced Beverly Heard to testify against former congressman Mel

Reynolds? Who "talked" Desiree Washington into filing charges against Mike Tyson?

Yes, Barry smoked crack, Mel liked young girls in uniforms, and Clarence was Vanesse Del Rio's number one fan, but that's not my point. I'm pissed at the man's use of Black women to bring down brotha after brotha and I'm tired of watching Black people get interrogated and judged by panels and panels of white men and women. And they say that everybody gets a fair trial.

Bullshit! Never in this country will you see the reverse of what has been witnessed. I don't care if it happens in Compton, East St. Louis, or Harvey, Illinois—no white person is ever going to get tried by a jury full of Black folks. Never! This has to change. If we're going to be fair, let's be fair. I'm tired of Black people getting the booty end of the stick.

I'm Concerned. Even though Mike is now considered a criminal, I want to see how many of his so-called friends stand by him. I watched a slew of white folks, who once praised him (the same ones he granted interviews to when their jobs were on the line), "flip" and cut him loose. But I'd expect that from them. Now, I want to see who is really a true friend to Mike Tyson, you know, the brothas—Eddie, Arsenio, Spike, Don King. I want to see what LL has to say. Friendship is the one thing Mike Tyson never had. His only friends came after he had 50+ million dollars. Let's see who's really down.

I'm Finished. I hate to sound like Nino Brown, but this is bigger than Mike Tyson. This is bigger than the Black thing and the white thing we always talk about.

This is a judicial, governmental, power structure thing that has to do with power. Don't think that it was a coincidence that Clarence Thomas and William Kennedy Smith got off and Mike got fked. There is a big difference between money and power. Thomas and Kennedy Smith had powerful friends in Washington. Tyson, however, well...

I'm Gone.

Exit Stage Left Even

Last month I learned a very valuable lesson. I watched Arsenio Hall's final show with that all-too-familiar half-ass smile that Black people display when we are in-between joy and pain. Tired of seeing him walk that multi-cultural "gray line," but genuinely sorry to see him go, I, like most other Black folks, watched the last two weeks of the Arsenio Hall Show like it was the Knicks vs. Bulls, Game 7.

Why was I interested in what Arsenio was going to do next? Why was he all of a sudden so important? Why did his shows get better after his cancellation was announced? Why was watching the show now the "Black" thing to do?

Blaxploitation or cancellation, which would you prefer? Arsenio Hall represented the good and the not-so-good of African American success. He stood tall as the only brotha with a late-night talk show, but honestly, the man's skinning and grinning was hard for real Black folks to take. The Night Thing was not always the right thing. The Arsenio Hall Show became the Black Ed Sullivan Show with Al Jolson as host. It showcased an incredible amount of Black talent. It also demonstrated that even people with the biggest hearts will sell a piece of their soul just to gain a nation-wide audience. Arsenio did this unconsciously.

One of the major problems with being Black in America is that you are required to be conscious at all times. The minute that white America says you are "too Black," the Black community turns on you and calls you a sell-out. It is the Hollywood Paradox. Your job as a Black man is to put as many brothers on as possible; your job as a man is to maximize as much of that American Dream as possible. Why can't Black folks do both?

In his brief run, Arsenio Hall did more good than bad. His failure to employ qualified African Americans in top positions overshadowed the fact that he gave considerable amounts of money to charities around the world. The fact that he consistently "fell all over" white women on that couch overshadowed the fact that he gave many unknown Black entertainers a vehicle to express their talents and views. The fact that he some-times tried too hard "not" to be Black in front of whites overshadowed the fact that he made sure the movie "Bopha" got completed and found national distribu-tion. If this was baseball, he'd be batting .500. But since it's life, he's become another brotha who's turned his back.

Think seriously: How many African Americans with fame, money, or power still reside in Black com-munities? How easy is it to give money to pseudo-Black organizations knowing that the Blacks who really need that money will never see it? How do Black "stars" find all the time in the world for Entertainment Tonight and

Barbara Walters, but never seem to have time to volunteer at a Black community center? How many African American celebrities are truly committed to being Black?

On the flip side, we, the Black public, are just as bad. We demand that they do these things, and we continuously remind them that whatever they do is not enough. We really don't have much at all, yet, we don't support what we got. Because of this Catch-22 we put ourselves and our "heroes" under, we lose positions that took us 400 years to get. And everyone wonders why being Black is so much like work. Just ask Arsenio.

Soul on Ice

JUST ANOTHER TALE
FROM THE DARKSIDE

Another shooting occurred on the west side of Blackville, USA. One more African American community infiltrated by crack, America's newest drug epidemic. Replace Black-on-Black crime with Black-on-Black love? Just Say No to reality.

The number of African American males attending college is declining. Niggas are stacked in jails like cattle. The unemployment rate for Blacks is now higher than it was in 1980. Brotha, can you spare a dime? Who loves you, baby? Brotherman, Brotherman, Brotherman.

What the hell is this? Black women are tired of seeing Black men rotting away on a Blackville street corner; Black men are not tired of blaming the white man for everything that has happened to us. Educators and politicans constantly discuss the importance of education and how social reforms will assist African Americans. Scholars are still talking the theory thing, and white people are still sitting back watching us make damn fools of ourselves. Listen to Boogie Down Production's "Material Love" and you'll hear the story: "Tell me what the fk am I supposed to do?"

Writing this essay is a young Black man who has survived the bullshit, and one who has done the necessary things to stay alive in Blackville, USA. Masters degree from one of the Black schools, role model-type for the Y.B.M., supporter of Chesimard, basically, a brother trying to do the right thing.

Everyday Tony Brown, John Johnson, Julian Bond, Oprah, *The Final Call*, the Urban League, Clarence Thomas, or somebody says something about the status of the Young Black Male, singing songs without solutions. "Black men are becoming an endangered species. Brothas be wastin' they lives away. African American men are incapable of sustaining the status of their white counterparts. Sorry, boy, you have no future."

Messages: stay in school, don't do drugs, stay off the streets, love thy neighbor, and all that. Yeah, right. What's a Black man supposed to do? Stay unemployed? All of the so-called African American leaders claim that many Black male adolescents need role-models. Yes, we need more of them. Where are they?

Mothers crying, babies dying...tell me what the fk am I supposed to do? Being overlooked and unappreciated have become daily occurrences in the lives of many Young Black Males. Where does the Black man draw the line between survival and responsibility? Children go to school to better themselves and to make their parents proud. Education, they say, education. Education is the key to either having a life or having a lifestyle. Why then is my mother so financially unhappy? Why are so many "children of education" watching their parents struggle to make ends meet? Why aren't Black-owned and operated organizations, companies, groups, or corporations making a concerned effort to take a chance on

A-Doing-The-Right-Thing-Young Black Male?

Do white boys go through this? Hell no! This is a Black thang. This is a problem that confronts Black America and only Black America. African Americans need to understand the importance of economic empowerment. African Americans who are in the position to help to increase the Black work force should do so. No excuses, no sob stories.

A Soul on Ice. Baby, that's nice. Brotha think twice. Tell me what the fk am I supposed to do? Get paid or flip burgers? Go to school then get paid the right way. Yeah, right. Who's got my back? Where are the opportunities? Where are the promises? Where is my future?

Beeper-boy, how ya livin'? Fat. School-boy, how are you living? Flat. Just keep doing the right thing young brotha. You don't need a car, food, or shelter to survive. Yeah, right. Many upper- and middle-class Negroes are indirectly making life very difficult for the Black youths who have chosen not to hustle. Yo buppy, hire somebody!

Unemployment eats away at the soul. There is no security without financial security. Self-esteem has no place in today's economics. There has to be an avenue for the Y.B.M. to travel that combats the road that is always open, accessible, and easy. Give us a chance or we'll give up on you. Which is fk'd up? Will somebody please tell me what the fk am I supposed to do?

Brothas Gonna Work It Out

NE LIFE.
A sea of heads.
Afros and fades, bald and braids.
Standing one way, one direction.
Looking for guidance, wisdom,
and relentless understanding.
Through the words of the many men who led us,
we found life.
We found love.
We found...understanding.

One life.
One million men.
Black men.
On a mission.
A mission from God—
because ultimately,
that's what the Black man is.
"What's up, G!?!"
Seriously.
And finally, somebody helped us understand
what being a "god" is all about.

Black man.
Obsolete?
Dangerous?
Single?
There's a need to find
a foundation in our lives.
Each one, reach some.
Reach some, teach many.
DC. Chocolate City.
Home of the extraterrestrial brotha.
Home of the foundation,
not the plantation.

The Million Man March will forever be the focal point of a generation of Black men who have fallen for everything because we have stood for nothing.

On this day, the day the "niggas" took over, Black life came to a halt. Before we find ourselves alone, brothas have to take the time to listen to other brothas about what WE have to do for each other.

No white boys, no white money, no white nothing! Sistahs allowed, but not invited. This was the Black thing that gave meaning to those T-shirts we used to wear. A nation of millions—and no holding back with every brotha from Conrad Worrill to Stevie Wonder to Malik Yoba to Jesse Jackson to Ayinde Jean-Baptiste. We experienced full Black representation, hearing many words, much promise, and the truth about our survival, our future, our life.

Never have so many brothas come together with such focus. Always looking for love in all the wrong places, Black men finally took a day to find love in the one place where all of us fail to look: ourselves.

Farrakhan told us exactly what we needed to hear, as did every other speaker on the stage. One life, it's yours.

We listened and absorbed knowledge. We refused to let Ted Kopple's white-ass tell us who to listen to or what to do. Not this day! Denounce Brother Minister? Never. Not this day! Any brotha who had the vision to see this day and work toward its fulfillment is not the brotha we turn against. Not this day, not ANY day!

This day was the most beautiful thing in the world. The sea of Black heads being filled with Black knowledge—Black understanding. When Reverend Ben Chavis told every brotha there to "introduce yourself to the brotha next to you, shake his hand, give him a hug," every second of every Black man's life (my life) seemed worthwhile. The pain and the lack of pride in being a Black man in Amerikkka was gone. From niggas to gods in one day. Too bad we only have one life to live.

BROTHA II BROTHA, BLACK ON BLACK, FACE II FACE

Everybody's concerned about the young Black male, but no one is doing a damn thing to help. Everyone has "answers" to our problems, but nobody asks us what we think needs to be done. All of us ain't G'in' (gang bangin'). All of us ain't on drugs, slangin' rocks, or in jail. All of us don't want to be Michael Jordan, and all of us can't rap (but we can jump! Ha!).

The problem with this newly-found interest in the Y.B.M. is that the main element of concern—Y.B.M.— has been excluded from the discussion. So, for all the young brothas out there, I decided to answer the questions that nobody took the time to ask:

Q. What bothers you the most about the status of the Y.B.M. in America?
A. Just us, meaning Black men. You know, all I hear are things about how fk'd up we are. I mean if it ain't on the news, or in the paper, then some female is talking about how she can't find a decent Black man. Now, I know

there are some decent brothas out here, but, there are a lot of us who aren't living right either. That's what bothers me. There are both good and bad brothers, but the bad always seems to overshadow the good. Therefore, people see us only in one way. You know, that whole monolithic thinking thing.

Q. What do you think can be done to change this?
A. A whole lot of things, but it's basically a fantasy. You know, before we live right, we have to survive. And whether anyone wants to believe it or not, this country is not set up for us to succeed, or survive.

Q. What do you mean by that?
A. Let me give you an example. Whites hate being around Black folks. Hell, they used to lynch us just for steppin' into their neighborhoods. Like, when intergration become law, white folks ran like roaches when the lights came on. They moved from the cities and built phat-ass, lilly-white suburbs. Then they came back with U-Hauls and stripped the inner-cities of everything of value, especially jobs. They moved their businesses to the great-white suburbs. They moved their retail establishments and movie theaters to "their" malls, leaving downtown business districts looking like Northeast Detroit the day after Halloween.

Now, what are young brothas supposed to do? Are we supposed to move to the freaky-white suburbs and get "jacked" by Stacey Koon? Are we supposed to travel four-hours-a-day just so we can apply for a job that we will never get? Are we supposed to believe that we can go to "their" banks to get a loan to start a business in our own community? Hell mfkin' naw!

Q. So what, give up?

A. Not at all. But we must stop the stupid shit we doing, like taking each other out, the dumb shit. We need to find a way to get our shit together.

Q. How important is self-esteem in the life of a Y.B.M.?

A. Self-esteem is the foundation of every child. Unfortunately, generations of Black folks have been stripped of the understanding necessary—an appreciation of our heritage, culture, and ancestory—for us to feel good about ourselves. All of our lives we've been told that we ain't shit. We get these messages daily, from the media, the educational system, the police, the Republicans, the Democrats, Madison Avenue, Hollywood, white churches, Oprah, the criminal justice system, and corporate America. After a while, we start believing the lie and acting like we have no value, no unity, no purpose. Things have gotten so bad that today, to the average brotha out here, a job alone brings self-esteem. We are not talking about being a lawyer or owning a business, we are talking about a bullshit job at Footlocker. I'm telling you if there was some way to guarantee the Black child an economic future...

Q. So it's a money thing?

A. Yes and no. Of course, money has a lot to do with the way things are in Black society, but it's other factors as well. Education, religion, and how we are raised all play a part in how we look at ourselves and look at each other. But a man is raised to believe that in order to be a man, he must provide for himself and his family. Let's be real, this is Amerikkka. Here, money and race run everything. Black people are the wrong color and broke.

Q. Racism. Is everything simply Black vs. white?
A. Yes.

Q. Do you feel the white man is responsible for the situation you are in?
A. Personally, I think the white man, aka "the system," is the primary reason Black people around the world are in the position they are in today. I mean, not to give white folks credit or anything, but they've found a way to keep us down for 400 years—so they ain't stupid. At the same time, I think it's weak to hold them responsible when we are constantly destroying ourselves. We've been messed over and are being messed over. But we're not doing anything to help ourselves either. As long as we remain somewhat dependant on the system, we're going to stay like this. You know what I'm sayin'?

It's a joint effort. The white man cannot be held responsible for the situation we are in, but he damn sure is to blame.

To Be Continued...

THE LIFE OF
A T-SHIRT

W ord is bond, I had it goin' on. All over America—Crooklyn to Compton, South Bronx to South Central—I was in demand, in the hand and against the Klan. "It's A Black Thing" was my name. I started a movement that saw friends of mine (slogans) become household words. My whole family (T-shirts) was getting paid! Yeah baby, I was livin' large.

I got into the consciousness of Black folks and began a mental revolution that was 30 years overdue. The mind of the Black man and woman didn't change after Asante dropped "Afrocentricity" or when Farrakhan took over the Nation. The mind of Blackness changed when I started appearing on people's chests. For years, I had been the solution to the argument about relating Black life to white people: IT'S A BLACK THING, YOU WOULDN'T UNDERSTAND! For "eons" brothas and sistahs have been wondering how to phrase and express me. Now, finally a damn T-shirt has made me come alive.

I begin to revel in my accomplishments. I'm in NY, in DC, in L.A., in Memphis, hell I'm even in Boston!

Larry Bird may put me on...wait a minute, I'm getting big-headed. I do videos, make cameos in Spike Lee movies, and Arsenio even uses me in his monologue. Blam!!! I'm in there like swimwear! I'm Oprah-large! I'm sellin' like Nike and pumped like Reebok!

I'm...wow, hold up. What happened? The lights just got dim. Where's Robin Leach? Naw, don't tell me...it can't be true...it has only been three years...you mean, I'm just a faddddd??

Goddamn, it's hot in here (cough). I ain't seen no fk'n daylight in years (cough, cough). What the hell year is it anyway? Yo, "X" what year is it? 1993!!! What happened? Oh, Cross Colours, Karl Kani, Walt Disney, ACAA, Cohart, Stussy, P.A.I.D., and Starter. You mean to tell me that I got "souled-out" because of new ideas? New slogans? What about my message, man? I was more than a T-shirt, I was a message. An eternal message! Wait...Malcolm why am I talking to you? You are everybody's dream. You're more than a message, you're a face, you're historical photographs and words—you're a man! You're bigger than us. You were on baseball caps. You had a movie and e'rything. Even Michael Jordan had you on...why are you in this drawer with the rest of us? Over-exposed. Damn. They sold me out and they wore you out. Welcome to Black America, my brotha.

Okay, that's my story. It's amazing how I look at my life and can easily compare it to yours. Look at me now, packed in a dresser drawer like a slave on a ship, forgotten and considered "played out" like the Black Panther Party and Affirmative Action. Look at me, my life is reduced to a slogan like MLK's "I Have A Dream."

What happened to power, conviction, and ideology? Am I really just a t-shirt? All my life I thought I was more than that. I thought I stood for something. I thought I would last forever.

"It's A Black Thing, You Wouldn't Understand" is my name. You haven't seen me in a while, but you think about me all the time. My friends who appear on T-shirts, sweatshirts, and caps are there to ignite conscious behavior and express consciousness—forever. We really try to be more than words. We try to, you know, make authors, create lawyers, and mold leaders. So in the future, please don't do my partners the way you did me. Realize that our existence is more than just a wardrobe—it should be a lifestyle. You should understand because your life is a Black thing.

WHAT BLACK PEOPLE
SHOULD DO NEXT!

• Leave all white people alone.
• Start accounts in Black banks (savings accounts only).
• Keep checking accounts in white banks so they won't get paranoid.
• Send every Black child to a Black university either for the first two years, or to visit during homecoming.
• Refuse to pay taxes on white manufactured products—then stop buying them completely.
• Demand the same insurance rates on store fronts as the Koreans and Asians get.
• Carry around baseball bats to let white people know that we won't accept them readily moving back into our communities.
• Always demand Black stamps.
• Leave all white people alone.
• Stop worrying about petty things, like what we call ourselves: African American, nigger, nigga, etc...Your ass is Black whether you like it or not!
• Only vote in elections that have qualified Black officials running for the betterment of Black people (read this again).
• Buy 40 oz's in white neighborhoods (you won't find

them there so you won't drink 'em).
• Build Afrocentric curriculums across the country to establish the self-education we need in order to survive.
• Understand the concept behind 40 acres and a mule, and apply it to today's situations.
• Stop buying books by Black authors who only publish through white publishing houses.
• Police our own state.
• Create a job or internship for every Black student in school, so that the chain of Black expertise is never broken.
• Leave all white people alone.
• Turn off Juan Williams, Rush Limbaugh, Carl Rowan, Rush Limbaugh, Ken Hamlin, Whoopi Goldberg, George Will, Darryl Gates, and Sam Donaldson.
• Toss out Richard Daley, Pete Wilson, Newt, Clarence Thomas, Rudy Giuliani, and Jesse Helms.
• Watch "Living Single" and "Roc."
• Stifle every other minority in America talking that "we in the same boat" shit. We ain't!
• Give Black doctors, lawyers, and dentists a chance to prove their work.
• Stop leaving money around the house when broke-ass niggas come to visit.
• Stop giving up on your kids so soon.
• Stop being so Black that you become unproductive and unemployed.
• Divest from government dependency.
• Pick our own role models, politicans and spokespersons.
• "Check" any Black woman who considers herself a bitch.
• Oh yeah, leave all white people alone.

Brotha's Gonna Work it Out: *True*, November 1995

are u Black?

Labels define us. For whatever reason we always categorize the Blackness in us as being something, anything but Black. So for the sake of argument (or to instigate one), here's a questionnaire designed to label every bone, thought or activity that defines what Black is. Are you an African-American, Negro, Revolutionary, or Nigga? Or are you just Black? The choice is yours.

1. How would you respond to getting pulled over by the police?
   a. "Damn, ain't there some serial killers named Jeffery or Joe you can mess with?
   b. "Officer, there must be some mistake."
   c. "I don't have a license! Did you ask Fred Hampton that before you broke into his crib and killed him, pig?!?
   d. "They ain't takin' my ass back to jail..." Clik-Clik...Boom!

2. What was your response to the Rodney King verdict?
   a. "No justice, no peace."
   b. "Rodney King should have done what the officers asked him to do."
   c. "You know, this means war!"
   d. "Damn, that TV in Macy's window look good... gotta have that."

3. How would you respond to someone stepping on your shoes?
   a. "That's alright my brother."
   b. "Why don't you watch where you're going, buster."
   c. "You lucky you ain't white."
   d. "Mutha..." Clik-Clik...Boom!

4. What type of music do you listen to?
   a. Frankie Beverly and Maze
   b. Michael Bolton
   c. "Black man has no time for song and dance."
   d. Mobb Deep

5. What do you drive?
   a. Camry
   b. BMW
   c. "white folks crazy."
   d. "anything niggas leave open."

6. What do you buy from the store most often?
   a. Food for the family
   b. Fade cream
   c. Ammunition for the struggle
   d. 40oz

7. How do you settle a dispute?
   a. With a hand shake
   b. With a bouncing check
   c. By any means necessary
   d. Clik-Clik... Boom!

8. Would you shoot your brotha over a pork chop?
   a. No
   b. Certainly not
   c. "I will never fight my brotha over swine flesh."
   d. "Depends if it's the last one."

9. What's your favorite movie?
   a. Malcolm X
   b. Driving Miss Daisy
   c. The Spook That Sat By The Door
   d. Menace II Society

10. What is your favorite TV show?
    a. Tony Brown's Journal
    b. Different strokes or Gimme A Break ("They're both great!")
    c. "Black man has no time for the image of the beast."
    d. The news, because you might see somebody you know.

11. How many kids do you have?
    a. 2-3
    b. None ("I use protection.")
    c. "I consider every Black child a child of mine."
    d. "Shit, I dunno? Ask they mammas."

12. How often do you say, "Niggas ain't shit!" ?
   a. "Only when disrespected"
   b. "I rarely use such profanity."
   c. "I don't refer to my people as niggers, just confused."
   d. "Shit, we ain't."

13. What would you say to President Clinton?
   a. "What is your plan to help African-Americans acheive equal footing economically in this country?"
   b. "Who does your hair? Is that an Afro you're wearing?"
   c. "Who do you really work for, and where do they live?"
   d. "Inhale muthafka and pass the joint. A'yo Prez, where da hoes at?"

14. When you are on a bus, you...
   a. Sit where you want
   b. Sit behind the driver out of fear
   c. Ride shotgun
   d. Refuse to give up your seat to an elderly woman until you can make your way to the back.

15. You make money by...
   a. Starting your own business
   b. Working for a company that wants to fire you
   c. Selling bean pies
   d. Taking somebody else's

16. Reason you have a beeper?
   a. "I own my own business."
   b. "So my boss can call me anytime he wants."
   c. "So my phone won't be tapped by the government (and so I know who wants to buy bean pies!)."
   d. "'Cause I don't own no phone."

17. You see an article of clothing you would like to own, you...
   a. Ask the person where they bought it
   b. Say you like it, then talk about them behind their back
   c. Ask if the Army Surplus has anymore
   d. say, "A'ight bitch run the jacket! And give up the Jordans too!"

18. Who in history do you respect the most?

a. Malcolm X
b. Clarence Thomas
c. Nat Turner
d. Tupac

19. How do you get from here to there?
    a. Drive your car
    b. In a cab... if they stop
    c. By any means necessary
    d. Carjack

20. How do you refer to Black women?
    a. Sistah
    b. Inferior
    c. Queen of my nation
    d. Hoe, bitch, hoochie, freak, etc...

21. Favorite book?
    a. The Isis Papers by Francis Cress-Welsing
    b. anything by Dempsey Travis
    c. How To Load An Automatic Weapon Vol. 1
    d. ―――――――

22. Favorite magazine?
    a. Emerge
    b. The New Republic and Playboy
    c. "You mean, where I keep my weapons?"
    d. Players and High Times

23. Elvis?
    a. "He's dead, dammit!"
    b. "I love him. He's the King!"
    c. "Over-rated, overweight, child-molesting, drug addict, thief.'
    d. Muthafk him and John Wayne!"

24. Sista Souljah?
    a. "I like what she says, but she needs to act on some of her
       stands."
    b. "She needs to be shot."
    c. "My future wife."
    d. "It ain't like she Lil' Kim or Foxxy Brown."

25. What would you say to a 300-pound white woman?

a. "No comment. Too easy (laugh)."
b. "You look great! Your husband isn't around is he?"
c. "You know your forefathers started all of this shit!"
d. "It's too late! Dick Gregory can't even save yo fat white ass!"

26. You live in a high-rise, how do you get someones' attention below?
    a. intercom
    b. cellular phone
    c. shout out, "Black Power brotha!"
    d. "I can't. Them damn gates on my windows always get in the way."

27. How often do you eat at an Arab Submarine shop?
    a. occasionally
    b. never
    c. "Do they have bean pies?"
    d. "You mean a day?"

28. Stray bullets?
    a. "Why is it that brothas who shoot never hit what they are aiming for?"
    b. "Is that a new movie or a new group?"
    c. "Brothas be shooting at the wrong target. Here brotha, let me show you what you should be shootin' at."
    d. "Shit, they don't bother me. I'm used to 'em. Besides they ain't gonna hit me anyway."

29. If you had $1million, what would you do?
    a. Start or increase your own business
    b. Donate it to the Republican Party
    c. Buy a van full of dynamite and pay someone to drive it
    d. Buy one car to drive around the block in.

30. How would you spend the last hour of your life?
    a. "Talking to my family."
    b. "Asking Ronald Reagan for forgiveness."
    c. "Creating the blueprint to end white supremacy."
    d. "I probably don't have an hour left."